A History of

First Encounters Between Indigenous Peoples and Newcomers from the East to Central Canada

for Educators

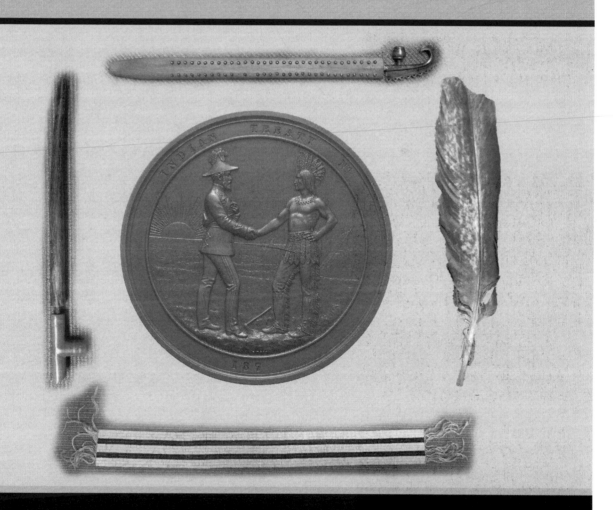

Brian Rice
University of Winnipeg

Kendall Hunt
publishing company

Cover images courtesy of Brian Rice

Kendall Hunt
publishing company

www.kendallhunt.com
Send all inquiries to:
4050 Westmark Drive
Dubuque, IA 52004-1840

Copyright © 2016 by Brian Rice

ISBN 978-1-4652-9025-0

Printed in the United States of America

TABLE OF CONTENTS

PREFACE

This book is primarily for educators who will teach Indigenous History and Culture to their classrooms. It includes some aspects of Indigenous Culture and then continues with encounters in history between newcomers and Indigenous peoples in the Americas with an emphasis on eastern Canada to the mid-west. I have included Indigenous perspectives on events before and then during particular times of contact. The first couple of sections of the book will help provide the reader with an Indigenous understanding of their origins and worldview. The rest of the book will incorporate, encounters from the 16th century including a special section on Columbus's voyages and his relationship with the *Taino* people in the Caribbean. The rest of the chapters are about pre-Canadian and post-Canadian encounters from 1534 to approximately 1880, except for a brief section on encounters prior to the United States becoming a country, the Americans being citizens of England until that time. It is from the areas inhabited by the colonists within the thirteen colonies that English Canada would derive with the United Empire Loyalists who chose to support the King of England and move north rather than separate.

Although this book will be primarily about the North American Indigenous worldview, and encounters between newcomers and Indigenous peoples and the pre- and post- Canadian experience, I included the section on Christopher Columbus and his voyages for a specific reason. It is during this early encounter with the Indigenous peoples of the Caribbean, that the beginnings of a global transformation would take place, especially concerning Indigenous peoples in the America's. This early encounter would set the stage for the legal, political, and social relationships that Indigenous peoples would have with Europeans and in particular concerning the rights Indigenous peoples would have to their lands in the Americas.

The 'preliminary' sections in the historical period will both give the historical context of the period and also help bring an understanding to the present day situation of Indigenous peoples in Canada. The second part of the chapters will include particular Indigenous peoples, their customs, and motivations during their first encounters with Europeans. In the book I have chosen to include a section on the historical development of Canadian government policies towards Indigenous peoples to further explain present day realities; therefore, this text isn't simply about the past, it is also about how we have arrived to the present. The main purpose of the book is to try and incorporate as wide ranging a perspective of historical events as possible.

Some of this book will be written as a recording of events; some of it will be ethnographic in content; and some of it will be written as narrative. The narrative approach and in particular chapters one and four allows more of an explanation for the Indigenous response during the first encounter, one during Columbus's voyages and the other the *Kenienke:haka* Flint People (Mohawk) and the French, most notably Samuel De Champlain. The Indigenous response in terms of their motivations towards one another is not neglected either. Indigenous peoples were sometimes in conflict with one another before the arrival of Europeans, which helped define their reasons for choosing different sides when there was confrontation with and among European nations.

Each chapter of the book leads into the next chapter and often includes parallel histories of certain events from a variety of perspectives. It is important that those who read this book will also read the journals and documentations of the first explorers, missionaries, and settlers as well. Hopefully, this book will help to widen the knowledge base of the reader and perhaps challenge some of the misconceptions about Indigenous peoples sometimes found in the historical record, which has been transmitted into the education system.

In order to provide as much of an Indigenous perspective as possible, the text includes a wide variety of place names and peoples in the Indigenous languages. This might be a little confusing for the reader at first; however, I have added an explanation as to how some Indigenous peoples received the names in use today. The reader will first see the name in the Indigenous language; then the literal meaning of the name in English or French; and finally the name in use in either historical texts or in use in the present day.

I hope you enjoy reading this book and that it will add to your knowledge base.

INDIGENOUS WAYS OF KNOWING

Introduction

In today's world, one of the most difficult aspects of Indigenous knowledge for the Euro-western community to come to terms with is Indigenous understandings about the world and their place in it. Significantly, Euro-western society has created methodologies about how the world came to be by way of a linear scientific and historical process that works well for the types of knowledges it recognizes. These methods aren't always the same for Indigenous peoples due to their different learning objectives and way of life. If as a society you objectify nature as a part of your worldview, then you probably believe that you are not dependent on it for survival. If your worldview includes nature as something to view subjectively, you probably believe in the interdependence of nature and your dependence on it for your survival. Indigenous ways of knowing include both survival skills and social skills that tie one directly in a relationship with nature. It also teaches proper conduct in how to live in a symbiosis relationship within the eco-systems Indigenous peoples live in. Although Indigenous knowledge and oral history is mostly cyclical rather than linear, there can also be a similar approach to contemporary events with that of Euro-westerners. Among the Cree for instance, there are two types of oral histories: *Atuikan* and *Tipachimun*. *Atuikan* oral traditions are those that tell of a time before human beings existed and when giant creatures roamed the earth. These are sometimes referred to as myths and legends; however, Cree elder Louis Bird referred to them as mystery stories because they have some truth but are not always fully understood because they come from a distant path. They explain why the earth became the way it is and that there are lessons for human beings to learn from the mistakes these primal beings made in the past. (Bird. 2000. personal correspondence) *Tipachimun* stories are the more recent stories that people remember of events taking place in this cycle of life and can be more easily validated. (Morantz. pp. 171–191) These stories mostly take place in more recent times and correlate with Euro-western understandings about history. This book will be mostly about *Tipachimun* type stories. However, it is important that readers understand some elements of *Atuikan* stories as well in order to understand the Indigenous world view of how things came to be.

How do Indigenous peoples pass on their knowledge?

Previous to colonization, for most Indigenous peoples, education was an informal way of being taught to understand the world they live in. In fact, the traditional education that Indigenous children received involved every facet of their lives. It included the development of relationships with everything that affects their lives in the natural world. This included relationships with each other, relationships with non- humans that inhabit the world, and relationships with beings that are beyond the physical world.

The first relationships developed were with the extended family and the people of the community. In some societies like the Ojibwa this includes a clan or *Dodem*. The *Dodem* is the link within the extended human family, the human and non-human families within the environment, and the non-human family outside the physical world. All three are linked. For people living in the northern hemisphere such as in Canada, the *Dodem* may be of an animal, for non-Ojibwa living further south, it may be a being from the plant world. This is part of the holistic outlook that Indigenous peoples possess that binds them to their environment. Oneida Professor, Dr. Pamela Colorado (1988 p. 50) says, "Indigenous science (knowledge) synthesizes information from the mental, physical, social, and cultural/historical realms. Like a tree the roots of Indigenous science (knowledge) goes deep into the history, body and blood of this land" meaning North America. The fact that much of the knowledge of Indigenous peoples comes from an oral tradition rather than a written tradition means innovative approaches must be created in order to synchronize the two traditions. Psychologist Jurgen Kremer (1995 p. 2) adds to this by asking, "Is there a way that Indigenous knowledge can be welcomed into academic discourse?" Unfortunately, because Euro-western ideas dominate the realm of knowledge, much of Indigenous knowledge including their oral histories have been invalidated and regarded as mythology or folklore. In any case; both Colorado and Kremer believe that it is essential to find a means that leads to understanding of Indigenous peoples and how they view their place in the world.

For instance, Ojibwa cosmology is divided between things that are animate or alive and those that are inanimate and not living. What is considered alive to an Indigenous person may not mean the same thing to a non-Indigenous person. Hence, a sacred pipe for the Ojibwa may be considered animate or a physical vessel in which life exists within. On the other hand a common smoking pipe would be considered inanimate.

In more traditional times, Children learned from an early age that they had a responsibility to others. Even before they entered the world, the learning process had already begun. Mothers began speaking and singing to their unborn children even while still in the womb. They began to share with the unborn child the lessons of life. They described for the child the different animals they would encounter. The Ojibwa felt that the soul of the baby was active and aware even before birth (Jenness pp. 90–95). These ideas and practices are presently endorsed to some degree by Euro-western medical practitioners who acknowledge that infants in the womb are quite aware of their surroundings before birth. Today it is not uncommon for many mothers of all backgrounds to sing to their unborn babies.

As Indigenous children began to grow up, they had to learn their responsibilities relative to other beings that are part of their world. For many Indigenous societies, it relied on putting the boys through a fast. The fast continued until, by way of a dream, the child learned about the non-human being that he is to have a relationship with for the rest of his life. Once found, the child honored this being throughout life. This was done through offering of feasts and prayers. Sometime it required keeping a part of this being in a sacred bundle. It was believed that in order to be successful in life a child had to develop a relationship with each of the animate aspects of creation – the human, the non-humans on earth and non- humans outside of the earth. Most of all, the child learned to develop a relationship with himself.

During a Native Studies symposium the late Cree/Ojibwa elder Peter O'Chiese was asked by a woman, how she could become more spiritual? Peter answered that she was already born a spirit. What she had to do was learn to become a human being. (University of Sudbury, 1996) According to my former colleague, Ojibwa elder Jim Dumont, (Traditional Teachings, 1992, University of Sudbury), when one learned to become a full human being, then they could say that they were *pimadisiwin* or living the good life, a life to the fullest, a 360 degree vision of the world.

The late, Cayuga chief, Jacob Thomas of the *Rotinonhsonni* said that when he was a youth, he was taught the proper way to walk and speak. The lessons he received in his youth helped him become a noted orator. Much of what he learned came from his grandmother. (Jacob Thomas. 1996. Traditional Teachings) Among the *Rotinonhsonni*, the grandmother on the maternal side of the family was an important influence on her grandchildren. Like the Ojibwa *dodem*, the *Owachira* or clan among the *Rotinonshonni* was very important. Thomas related a story that when he was a boy he went out with a girl from his community. His grandmother told him that she was a cousin on the maternal side of family and was a member of the same *Owichera*. Jake then had to leave this girl and find another. Unfortunately, Jake then went out with another girl, only to find out the same thing about this girl. Jake said his grandmother knew all of the extended relations of his *Owachira*. On his third attempt he got lucky. He also said that it was important that you don't marry someone closer than a fourth cousin on either the maternal or paternal side of the *Owachira*. Grandparents and grandmothers in particular are there to remind children of the proper way to conduct themselves in the society and to guide them through their adolescence.

People are not the only beings with whom Indigenous peoples are required to develop relationships with and show proper conduct towards. For instance, there are still places that require the sacrifice of tobacco. These places are considered animate in some traditions. When Indigenous peoples make offerings in such places, they are showing respect for the generations that walked in these places before them as well for those who have passed away and now live in the beyond. These places have energies that can be tapped into and can bring good fortune or bad fortune depending on the amount of respect shown. Oral traditions often told how these places came to be. Some were formed out of the entities of the past.

For Indigenous peoples of North America, learning was experiential and children were never physically reprimanded for doing something wrong. In the past, Indigenous families were criticized by the Christian clergy for not using corporal punishment and for allowing children too much freedom. It is only in recent years that corporal punishment is now seen as a detriment to society by most non-Indigenous North Americans. However, with freedom came social values that were taught. For example, there was always someone in the extended family who could take care of a child if there was a problem or who could direct a child if there was a mistake made. Likewise, children were taught if they made a mistake, they alone had to take responsibility for their actions. Therefore, it was essential that they received instruction from all members of the extended family. In the *Rotinonshonni* language, the word mother – ista – refers to every woman in the clan. Each woman has a responsibility in the upbringing of the children in her clan.

Who were the Indigenous teachers?

Those who were the teachers of Indigenous children were also the ones who had the most knowledge. These people are the Elders, both men and women, and they play a significant role in the lives of Indigenous children. They have wisdom and experience that they can pass on. Usually this knowledge has been passed down through many generations. Sometimes these Elders belong to ancient societies. In the North East to the west of North America this knowledge was passed on in the winter by way of oral traditions. This was when the physical aspects of mother earth was covered in snow and her body came to rest. In the *Ojibwa* culture these stories of how the world came to be are still referred to as *Atisokan* (*Atuikan* in Cree) ancient stories and were recounted to the young. More common stories are known as *Tibajimowan* (*Tibachimun* in Cree) historical stories. It is during these harsh winter times that the children learned about the seven teachings: courage, respect, love, humility, truth, wisdom and honesty. They may also learn that the bear represents courage, the buffalo-respect, the eagle-love, the wolf-humility, the turtle- truth, the beaver-wisdom, and the Sabé Bigfoot – honesty. These teachings are still relevant today and are being incorporated into the modern Education system.

Family members and elders also belonged to sacred societies where knowledge was passed on. These were called *Nanidawi, Wabano, Jeesakeed,* and *Midewiwin*. However, it is the *Midewiwin* that is the most prevalent society in existence today. It is still open to all persons of *Anishnabé* descent. That includes the *Ojibwa,*

Chippewa, Potowotomie, Odawa, Saulteau, and *Algonquin* and some invited members of other Algonquian speaking Indigenous North American societies. Through the rituals, songs and stories, the initiate becomes an integrated part of the *Ojibwa* cosmology. Foremost for the *Midewiwin* is knowledge of herbs and medicines. Essential to the rite of passage into this society is the death and rebirth of the initiate. Usually this involves a transition from a novice level into a new and sophisticated level of development. Once this occurs, the person proceeds to a lifetime of learning and reaching of the different levels of knowledge which correspond to the four levels of the cosmology that are below and above mother earth.

In *Ojibwa* cosmology the three types of beings human, non- human on earth and non- human spirit are natural processes that work together as one. As well, it is important that one knows there are many Indigenous men and women who are not a part of any society who have important knowledge to pass on. These teachers carry knowledge that is extremely important. Like the sacred places where offerings are made, it is a requirement when receiving such knowledge to offer tobacco to the person sharing the knowledge. This is out of respect for both the person and the knowledge that he and she has and is offering. When visiting an elder it is important that you bring something of value in exchange. If all you can afford is a piece of cloth, then that has as much value as a fur coat that a richer person might offer. The person who has the knowledge will know if the recipient is sincere or not.

It is important to understand that when dealing with traditional knowledge that involves non-human entities, a person with bad intentions will receive benefits only a short time. In the Indigenous understanding of life, everything comes full circle or *enjiné*.

There are also practical everyday knowledges such as survival skills to be learned. This requires showing proper respect for the land and animals. This among many other important lessons means learning how to track, hunt and trap animals and tan their hides. A Cree social studies text entitled (*Cree Trappers Speak.* Pp. 9 to 15) indicates that it is the *nitibaaihtaan* or tallyman who is responsible for seeing that these things are fulfilled. He sets the beaver quotas so that they can be safely harvested as well as the dates for trapping. He knows that at the end of March, beaver traps have to be removed from the water due to the fact that the females are pregnant. He also makes sure that the trappers remain within their boundaries. If one of his trappers moves into another's territory and discovers a new beaver lodge, it is up to him to inform the *nitibaaihtaan* of the area. The Cree refer to a person which is a good hunter as *naabaaw*. In the chart form below, what constitutes a good leader and hunter are noted. These values can also be used in everyday life:

A GOOD HUNTER	A GOOD LEADER
– does not boast	– is a good hunter
– never causes others embarrassment	– teaches by example
– never speaks about how he killed an animal	– consults others and values their opinions
– conducts himself with dignity and restraint	– excercises leadership
– reveals information about his hunt slowly and often without words	– obtains consensus among his hunters
– shows modesty	
– shares with others	
– when game is scarce is still able to catch something	

The values of the *Rotinonshonni, Ojibwa* and *Cree* teachings are important for teachers and other professionals to understand. In a society that emphasizes the individual they may not understand why children from

Indigenous societies don't always put themselves forward: cooperation trumps individualism. Respect comes from being humble. As a former physical education teacher in an *Anishnaabé* school, my students when playing sports rarely counted score. The sport of the game and cooperation between players was often more important to them than the end result. The person who was the best player never bragged but was honored by the others. The seven values of the *Ojibwa* and the traditional Cree teachings are earned by how others look at you and not how one promoted oneself or in this case didn't promote themselves.

What are some of the obstacles Indigenous Peoples face in passing on their knowledge?

Cayuga Chief and elder, the late, Jacob Thomas commented on changes he has witnessed in this century with respect to how knowledge is passed on. He said that when he was a boy, there was no television, radio, automobiles, or even telephones. Elders from other communities would visit his family. They stayed for months at a time because it was difficult to travel. They would sit and tell stories all day long or they would go to the ceremonial Longhouse and practice learning ceremonies. The children would always be welcome. They would then practice what they heard and saw themselves. Sometimes the Elders would call them over and let them practice with them. There were long speeches to memorize as well as elaborate rituals and protocol to be learned. In itself, the ceremony for elevating someone to the level of chief took about ten hours. (Jacob Thomas.1996. Jacob Thomas Learning Center)

Thomas also commented on what he observed in these present times. Due to varied and improved transportation options, people often visited and left the next day. Children are also preoccupied with new and different activities such as watching television in contrast with practicing ceremonies and learning their culture. The biggest change, however, is in the relationship between the young and the elderly. Today Elders are often relegated to live in old age homes while, at the same time, the young are put into daycare centers. This way there is no chance for a true relationship between those who are the most knowledgeable and those who are of the age of learning. (Jacob Thomas. 1996. Jacob Thomas Learning Centre)

With out a doubt, one of the most dramatic effects on Indigenous systems of learning in North America was the Residential schools and Industrial schools. This system of education, imposed on Indigenous children in Canada and the United States was highly destructive to the Indigenous way of life and learning. The taking away of Indigenous children from their families has resulted in children returning to their community's years later with little knowledge of their languages, traditions and history. This has had a great impact on Indigenous communities throughout North America and most in particular, Canada. With these schools there was rampant physical and sexual abuse while children were indoctrinated in a Christian and Euro-western worldview that had little to do with their home life. Although the Residential Boarding School system has been abolished in both Canada and the United States, its effects are still lingering with Indigenous adults who attended and passed the abuse they received onto their children. Fortunately, there has been a revival by the youth in learning their culture, languages and ceremonies and at the same time receiving a western education.

How are Indigenous people: integrating traditional ways of knowing with modern education?

Over time, Indigenous peoples in North America have had to adapt to drastic changes. This has required finding new ways of utilizing and preserving their traditions. Today most Indigenous North Americans have gone through the formal Euro-western education system. Many are utilizing the system to enhance their knowledge. Many have entered the professional fields. Some of these fields such as education and social work have incorporated Indigenous teachings into their curriculum. It is even mandatory in some institutions in Canada, that non-indigenous persons take courses on Indigenous issues and culture. Indigenous professionals are finding ways of incorporating the traditional with their contemporary ways of living to the benefit of others. Many have faced great adversity in their lives in trying to achieve their goals and they have succeeded in becoming doctors, lawyers, teachers, professors, business professionals without sacrificing their Indigenous identity. With respect to formal education Cayuga chief, the late, Jacob Thomas only had a grade five education, yet he taught for fourteen years at Trent University. Specifically, he had taught the history and culture of the *Rotinonshonni*. This fortunate situation occurred because an institution of higher learning recognized his expertise in the area. However, situations like Jacob's have been far from the norm. In other areas of life where traditional education is normally taught, Elders who have lived all of their lives in the forests of northern Canada or in the arctic are often required to take courses in wildlife management if they want to continue to trap and hunt. They are often taught by young formally educated persons who have spent little time in the wilderness.

We will finish this section with a speech that reflects these ideas and that was taken down in the eighteenth century. It was delivered by a leader of the *Rotinonshonni* named *Canassatago* who was speaking to missionaries who wanted to take his children from their home and communities to be educated. Notice the disregard for the education of female children where in a society like the *Rotinonshonni* both genders were equal whereas in Euro-Canadian and American societies, they were not until the twentieth century, this was a step back and not forward:

We know you highly esteem the kind of learning taught in Colleges, and the maintenance of our young men, while with you, would be very expensive to you. We are convinced, therefore, that you mean to do us good by your proposal; and we thank you heartily. But you who are so wise must know that different nations have different conceptions of things; and you will not therefore take it amiss, if our ideas of this kind of education happens not to be the same with yours. We have had some experience of it. Several of our young people were formally brought up in the colleges of the northern provinces; they were instructed in all of your sciences; but were bad runners, ignorant of every means of living in the woods, unable to bear either cold or hunger, knew neither how to build a cabin, take a deer, or kill an enemy, spoke our language imperfectly, were therefore neither fit for hunters, warriors, nor counselors, they were totally good for nothing. We are however not the less obliged for your kind offer, tho' we decline accepting it; if the gentlemen of Virginia shall send us a dozen of their sons, we will take great care of them, and instruct them in all we know and make men of them (Canassatego in Blanchard p. 127).

Name: _____   Time: _____

Learning Activity

1. Who were the most influential teachers that you knew when growing up?

2. What rites of passage did you experience as you progressed from childhood to adulthood?

3. Are the values that you learned growing up comparable that of the Ojibwa and Cree?

4. What are some of the changes you have seen concerning over the years concerning Indigenous peoples.

Review

1. What are some of things Indigenous children are required to learn?

2. What are the ways in which Indigenous peoples passed on their knowledge?

3. What are some of the contemporary problems Indigenous peoples have in retaining their knowledge?

4. How have Indigenous peoples adapted to changes from the traditional ways to contemporary ways of knowing?

References

Blanchard, David. (1980). *Seven Generations: A history of the Kanienkehaka*. Kahnawake; QU. Kahnawake Survival School.

Bird, Louis. (2000). Personal Correspondence. University of Winnipeg

Colorado, Pamela. (1988). Bridging Native Science with Western Science. Convergence, XX1, p–50.

Cree Trappers Speak. (1980). James Bay: Waskaganish Education.

Dumont, Jim. 1992. Traditional Teachings. Personal Correspondence,

Native Studies, University of Sudbury

Grimm, John. (1983). *The Shaman: Pattterns of religious healing among the Ojibwa Indians*. Norman and London: University of Oklahoma Press.

Jenness, Diamond. (1935). The cycle of life and death (Chapter IX) The Ojibwa Indians of Perry Island: Their social and religious life. Anthropological Series #17, Bullitan No.&8. Ottawa: National Museum of Canada, pp. 90–95.

Kineitz, Vernon. (1981). *The Indians of the Western Great Lakes* 1615–1760.

University of Michigan Press: Ann Arbor Paperbacks.

Morentz, Toby. (1984). Oral and recorded history in James Bay. In William Cowan (Ed) *papers of the fifteenth Algonquin Conference*. Ottawa: Carlton University. Pp. 171–191.

Thomas, Jacob. (1996). Traditional Teachings. Personal Correspondence, Jacob Thomas Learning Center. Oshewegan: Ontario

ORIGINS (Stories of how Indigenous Peoples came to be) AND THEIR PLACE IN THE LEARNING CYCLE OF LIFE

Introduction

Educators should first and foremost understand that Indigenous peoples have their own understandings of where and how they originated and how they interpret their history. Rather than always being fixated on dates and sequential time periods as markers of their beginnings, Indigenous peoples are concerned about how the social fabric of their society developed from its inception and how they continue to evolve into contemporary times. These stories are related from oral traditions centered upon the environments in which Indigenous peoples live. Often they tell of a time that predates humanity when other creatures much larger and more powerful lived upon the earth. These beings were viewed as the ancestors of the beings that inhabit the earth with us today. Out of the demise of these first beings came the world we now live in and within that world evolved the human being who in many oral traditions is the last being created. Some Indigenous societies in North America believe that when this world passes out of existence, the cycle of life will continue in new forms. Indigenous creation stories are about the regeneration of both the world and the environments within and the dependency human beings have on them for our own survival and that is the crux of these first oral traditions of coming to be.

How do Indigenous peoples understand their places of origin?

According to Euro-western scientific theories, the world came into existence some 4.5 billion years ago. Dinosaurs, the first reptiles to inhabit the earth disappeared some 65 million years ago. In its first form, the human being began to evolve some two million years ago, while modern humans began to appear some 250,000 years ago and continues to evolve today. However, this book isn't concerned with the Euro-scientific view as there are better sources than this to find this information out. One thing to note, while there is a great deal of speculation, the evidence linking modern humans and the first humanoids that appeared two million years ago is still unfolding. An Indigenous understanding of the story of the disappearance of the dinosaurs has to do with a story about creation and how the reptiles were put under ground by the creator so they wouldn't harm the new born human beings. They are never to be taken up as they will cause sickness and disease. The thunders or in some traditions the thunderbirds are responsible in keeping these creatures from doing harm to the earth. Aren't fossil fuels the remnants of these long past living entities.

Discrepancies in modern science are left to theoreticians to come up with ideas as to what those links are. Theory itself comes from the Greek word *theoria* which means to view from the outside. "Theory is a way of looking at the world and not a form of knowledge of how the world is" (Henderson. 1992. P 2). Since Darwin's theories of evolution in the nineteenth century, Euro-western scientists have put forward theories that have tried to find links between creatures from different time periods. According to one theory, human beings are believed to be off shoots of primates even though there is no clear evidence of a direct link as of yet. The world itself is thought to be in a process of continual development as it moves from primitive to modern.

Before the existence of modern human beings, it was believed that all life existed in a state of continual flux. The world existed with no social interaction among its different creatures. In fact, it is only recently that Euro-western science has suggested that humankind evolved out of a more primitive state into a more advanced one eventually culminating into our present day civilized society. It was also believed by evolutionists that there were still people living within the early stages of humankind that could be studied as to how human beings evolved. These were the Indigenous tribal peoples whose belief systems were said to have not yet advanced out of the primitive stage of mythology into the advanced stage of science. According to the perception created about Indigenous peoples in the America's, they were unable to separate themselves from their superstitious understandings about how life came into existence. Moreover, they were not advanced enough to look at the world objectively. This would only occur when they became educated enough to break the yoke that held them back from advancement. That yoke being their culture. When this happened they would be able to take their place in the modern world.

Many Euro-western scientists believe that out of the world of advanced technology would come the solutions to the world's problems such as poverty, hunger, warfare, and disease. Unfortunately, recent history is not always proving them right. The response they profess has been studies showing that we are better off now than we have ever been in the past. However, most of these studies include only peoples from Europe and not humanity as a whole. For peoples from European based societies, thanks to the lands and resources of Indigenous peoples in other parts of the world, this is probably true. For those exploited by European expansionism, it is not the case for the Indigenous peoples of America and especially for our non-human relations. Even the discussion about poverty comes from a Euro-centric paradigm and not an Indigenous one based on how much monetary wealth one has to feed oneself. For most of human existence money was non-existent and therefore, non-essential. An example being on the Prairies, with 50 million bison, there was an insurmountable food source for the smaller Indigenous societies that lived off of the land and animals. At the same time people were starving in European countries. In the east and south of North America, corn fields were said to stretch for miles along with beans and squash. Both sweet potatoes and potatoes were in abundance. There was also an abundance of fruits to live off of including strawberries, blueberries, raspberries, plumbs and cranberries. During the spring maple trees were tapped for nourishment. In the north fur was used for making clothes whereas cotton was weaved in the south, something relatively unknown in Europe. All of these agricultural products were unknown in Europe before the arrival of Columbus. Even the Tomato was new with Europeans refusing to eat them until several hundred years later believing they were a food from the devil. Water was another resource that although available in Europe had been poisoned resulting in many waterborn diseases and when Europeans arrived in the Americas, they preferred beer fearing deadly diseases such as Cholera. If we go even further south, trees were tapped for rubber, pineapples and bananas were grown, and cocoa plants produced chocolate while others produced vanilla. Most of all there was little disease until the arrival of Europeans meaning there was little worry about dying from bacterial contagions. After the arrival of Europeans to the Americas there was a catastrophic decline of Indigenous peoples due to diseases brought from Europe, as much as 90 percent of the population. (Jennings p. 28)

Indigenous peoples also hold another view about their traditions. They believe that some events in the world are so incomprehensible to the human being, that it is a great wonder and mystery to them. So rather than have an anthropomorphic deity in their stories of creation, they prefer to view it as a mystery that can't be solved which includes both human and non-human forms of life. However, those stories that did evolve from the past that include certain deific manifestations are there to teach moral lessons about how we should conduct ourselves in the world. If we don't heed the lessons in the stories it could be disastrous for both humans and non humans who reside together in the world. A part of their worldview is that Indigenous peoples have a responsibility to those forms of life that allow them to survive and flourish.

They are reminded of their responsibility by some of their oral traditions which tell about a time when human beings became powerful and arrogant about their place in the world order. They mention a technologically superior order of existence that predates humankind as we know it. The Ojibwa have a story about an advanced society destroyed by a flood because they lost their moral teachings on how to live in the world. Others such as the Mayans and Lakota believe that they had their beginnings on an island in the east which sank. It was on this island that a great society once flourished (Ross p. 60).

The story of the flood is a central theme for many Indigenous societies throughout the world. The Hebrews, tribal ancestors of the Jewish people, believed that under the instructions of Jehovah, a person named Noah gathered as many animals as he could find into pairs and placed them in a large vessel. He found land by sending out doves to search for it. In the Hebrew tradition, Noah is attributed with saving the remaining creatures of the world. The assumption that Noah had a special place in the story of the salvation of the living creation, has been incorporated into the religious belief systems of Euro-western society and much of the world. This includes the religions of Christianity and Islam.

The *Anishnaabé, Rotinonshonni* and many other Indigenous societies in North America also have a story about the flood but with a fundamental difference. In their stories, it is through the intervention of the animals that the world is saved so that human beings can inhabit it. It is a belief that the human being is the most dependent creature of all forms of life, and therefore needs the animals and other forms of life for food, clothes, shelter in order to continue to exist. Some *Anishnaabé* understand their name as meaning humble human being, in order to understand their place in the cycle of life. This is a fundamental philosophical difference in comparison with the Euro-western view of creation which maintains that human beings, in particular men are dominant in the order of creation. This is contrary to the Indigenous belief that mother earth which provides all living things with her life giving properties, is essential to their survival, and therefore, as important as any male anthropomorphic being. The belief in a male dominant creative agency, has affected the relationship that Euro-North Americans have to the natural world. In recent years, as technology has advanced, Euro-western men have become more confident in their sense of dominance. Only recently have Euro-western women been allowed to assert themselves, something Indigenous women have always done.

One way to understanding their place in the natural world, especially during times of natural catastrophe, Indigenous North Americans had tricksters and sacred clowns to help them cope during times of difficulty. These figures had their beginnings in the stories about creation. Among the Ojibwa, *Nanabush* stories are filled with the sometimes comical experiences of this mythical figure. The *Lenni Lenapé* referred to him as *Misabos*, The Great Hare, while other Indigenous North Americans like the Navaho referenced him as a coyote. In the *Atisokan* stories of the Ojibwa, *Nanabush* is a benevolent being of the highest order who is personally involved in the creation of the world. Even so, he/she continually finds themself in comical situations due to the unpredictability of events. Often in these stories *Nanabush* is fooled by the other animals. The reason for this is to remind the Ojibwa that there is always uncertainty about how much control anyone can have over the events of creation. These stories are also a reminder that even the greatest beings in the order of creation are fallible. They believe that mother earth can go through sudden changes in a moments' notice such as happened with the great flood and will do so again.

Indigenous North American origin stories tell us about events that occurred long ago. They speak about a time when the creatures that roamed the earth were larger than the animals we know today. They also tell of a humanoid like being who lived among humans who was larger and hairier in appearance, a time when the earth was covered with ice that would kill mother earth only to have her reborn every year and a time when the earth was consumed by a flood. Some of these stories fit with the evidence of some of the scientific theories of today. Where they differ is that they are more concerned with the meaning of life in a process of relationship to one another including the human being than simply the disconnected physical components that make up the world. These stories are there to help us live a good life, in Ojibwa *Pimadsiwiwn*, and to show us that we are all connected. In *Lacota* the term is *Mitakuye Oyasin* "We Are All Related", and that is what makes them important.

What is the connection between an Indigenous meaning of origin and the scientific view of how our solar system was formed?

In the Ojibwa creation story as written down by *Midewiwin* elder Eddie Benton Banai (1979 pp. 1–4), we are told that before the universe was formed, there was silence and darkness. However, a sound began to emanate from the somewhere in the centre of the void and then carried outward. In the centre where the sound began was the creator of all things. This is referred to as the first fire of the teaching. If we look at this same idea from a Euro-western scientific point of view, it suggests the Big Bang Theory, a theory that hypothesizes a primary explosion as the beginning of the universe. The Creator than sent out his thoughts in every direction, leaving stars and light in a flaming circle. Thus the second fire of creation. Again we might equate this in Euro-western scientific terms with the galaxy which when looked at from afar appears as a spiral circle. From the circle of fire came all of the qualities that bring life including the seasons, winds, directions, the sun and the moon. This is called the third fire. This suggests the beginning of our solar system. Next in the Ojibwa creation story came the circular motion of the universe. This can be likened to the orbit of the planets. This is the fourth fire. Benton speaks of the arrival of winged creatures and the fifth fire. There are scientists who theorize that the dinosaurs evolved from winged feathered creatures. Then earth, a woman with raindrops for her tears and lakes and streams for her blood was created. From her body evolved all forms of life. This is the sixth fire. Finally, the creator took handfuls of dirt from Mother Earth. In some stories it is said he blew into a shell. This is the seventh fire. It is believed by scientists that man's physical body began to evolve from micro-organisms and had continued to evolve into its present form. *Midewiwin* elder and former colleague in Native Studies, Jim Dumont, says the Ojibwa creation story takes about seven days to recite. The version offered by Banai is therefore an abbreviated one.

By comparison, in the *Rotinonshonni* creation story the world consisted of only water. The water fowl and water bearing animals were the only ones to be able to survive. Loon was looking down and saw the reflection of a woman coming from below. Heron looked up and told the others that she was coming from the sky. The water fowl flew up and provided a cushion for the woman to lie on. The other water bearing animals, otter, muskrat, beaver and turtle said they would offer their backs so that the woman would have a place to reside on. Each tried and failed until turtle made the attempt. He was strong enough to hold her and he would expand to provide more room. Still, there was something lacking. The animals then said they would look for earth below the water, because without earth the woman couldn't flourish. Each made the attempt and the weakest of all, muskrat, was the only one who reached the bottom and brought up some dirt. The story goes onto tell about how each contributed to the replenishing of the world so that human beings would one day be able to survive.

The story continues that the world was one land mass surrounded by water. *Teharonhia:wako* Holder Of The Heavens or creator divided the land into haves and then quarters Euro-western society supports a s story about continental drift. It also tells about when *Sawiskera* He Brings The Ice, populated the earth with lizards and other monstrous creatures. These were placed in a cave under the earth during a time of freezing and when it was over *Teharonhia:wako*, repopulated with mammal type creatures and finally humans.

David Cusick an Indigenous Tuscarora in 1812, put down a story of how after *Teharonhia:wako* created humans, his brother created apes. This was a story written down long before anyone knew about Neanderthals and Cro-Magnan man, at a time when Europeans still thought the world was only 6,000 yrs. old. This story also predates Darwin's theory of evolution. The Cree also have stories of battles with hairy humanoid creatures and even mammoths. (Beauchamp pp. 2–5)

It isn't important for someone reading this story to believe in all of the details that occurred in it. The story isn't theirs and therefore it isn't important that they believe in it. It is more important to understand why Indigenous peoples view nature in the way they do. They see it making sacrifices so that human beings can survive. In return, human beings must reciprocate by making offerings and participating in ceremonies of thanks for all they have done for them. In other words we are all a part of nature and not separate from it.

In many Indigenous stories about the creation of the human being, the physical component comes from the earth, The Creator blows a living spirit into it and the human being is born. In fact all newborns begin life when they take their first breaths. As well, the earth is considered feminine and from her all physical life evolved. The sun, on the other hand, is considered masculine and like the fertilizing seed of the male, helps begin the process of life by impregnating the earth with its rays. This first begins with the plant life and new species evolve, the cycle continues. The moon is the grandmother, and she controls both the tides and the women's cycle. The lunar cycle of many Indigenous societies follow the thirteen periods of the female menstruation cycle during the year, without this feminine aspect of creation there can be no renewal.

These stories are rational in their analysis of how life evolved. Moreover, they offer a living human context of understanding. Where they differ from the Euro-western scientific explanation is in their holistic understanding as to what constitutes life. For example, the *Rotinonshonni* believe the human being is made of both matter and spirit, that there is a living energy in the physical body that remains in the body for sometime even after death that renews life. These energies are not believed to be valid by Euro-western scientists. However, when we really look at it from an Indigenous perspective we can better understand the truth to this teaching. In the *Rotinonshonni* tradition when someone dies, it is important that they are buried in the earth within three days and no pollutants be included. This way it is ensured that new life will be born from the decomposing body. That is the energy that brings new life to the world. That living energy allows us to be natural regenerators of life and we are simply reborn into new forms of life.

When Euro-western scientific beliefs are compared with Indigenous ones, we can identify significant similarities between the two. However, Euro-western science does not acknowledge the areas of energies or spirit as valid even though in private many scientists will tell something different. Indigenous people believe that the living energy in the physical body can regenerate life and that this ability exists in other forms of life as well. While the two schools of thought agree on the ideas of decomposition and regeneration, they differ in their views on how energy survives after the physical body perishes. For Indigenous peoples a belief in a living energy in all things in life and in death as a natural part of their reality is so ingrained in their world view that they see its proof in everyday existence. This is the reason *Rotinonshonni* tradition requires that they wake up with the sunrise to give thanks for all of the gifts that the natural world brings to them. This has to do with their understanding as to what constitutes life. Rather than simply a product of particles and substances, the sun as it rises and provides warmth, is proof of its living energy.

How do Indigenous understandings of origins conflict with a Euro-western understanding of origins?

Indigenous notions of understanding and those of Euro-westerners have not had an alliance over the years. In many ways, they have seemed to be at opposite ends of the spectrum. In the past, Euro-western scientists, religious institutions, and academics have been direct participants in the destruction of Indigenous cultures, peoples and knowledge systems. Most notably this has occurred in the Americas. It is still going on in other parts of the world.

Writer and historian Robert Berhofer in his book the White Man's Indian gave an overview of the influence that Euro-western science and anthropology has had in the destruction of Indigenous societies in America.

He writes on the influence that Charles Darwin's theory of evolution as presented in Darwin's publication *On the Origin of Species by Means of Natural Selection, or the Preservation of Favoured Races in the Struggle For Life* has had on modern scientific thought. (Berkhofer pp. 49–52) This theory is based on the principle of natural selection or preservation of favoured races in the struggle for life. Responding to Darwin's idea, other social scientists suggested that evolution was a catalyst in a whole new way of understanding the development of peoples and societies, but based on an older religious premise of their being chosen peoples. Acceptance of Darwin's theory meant that peoples and their cultures came to be measured on an evolutionary scale that focused on technological progress. In the mid-nineteenth century, Louis Henry Morgan, the father of modern ethnology, was one of the first to utilize this new science in the study of the *Haudenosaune* also known as *Rotinonshonni*. He classified all societies using labels such as lower, middle, and upper savage; lower, middle, upper barbaric; and finally civilized. On his scale of evolution, Indigenous societies were anywhere from middle savage to middle barbaric while European societies were civilized. (Berkhofer p. 53).

The repercussions for Indigenous peoples were serious in that on the evolutionary scale they were at lower levels both culturally and biologically. This meant that they were viewed by the Euro-western scientific community as biologically closer to the cavemen and ape species. Along with this came the beginning of physical Anthropology where race became the measure of evolution. Again, in the mid-nineteenth century, Samuel George Morgan suggested that by measuring skulls of persons from different races, he could draw conclusions about the superiority or inferiority of different peoples. Since a European skull he believed was larger than skulls from non-Europeans, this showed that they were superior (Berkofer p. 58).

The implications of these studies were disastrous for Indigenous North Americans in that the policies made by the governments of the United States and Canada in the nineteenth and early twentieth centuries were rationalized because of these discoveries about race. In the United States, this led to Manifest Destiny which was the American view that advanced races inherited the right to take over the lands and resources of less advanced races. The Canadian form of this same idea came in 1876 as the Indian Act, which meant that Indigenous cultures in Canada had to be replaced with advanced Euro-western forms of culture. Although this became a premise that came out of science, it was rooted in theological assumptions about non-Christians and what rights they held to their lands (see doctrine of discovery chapter three). Policies such as this resulted in Indigenous North Americans removed from their lands and their children taken away for advanced learning.

The fact that many Indigenous societies refused to submit to these policies and tried to hold onto their cultures only further proved to bureaucrats that Indigenous peoples were incapable of raising themselves to the same level as the higher races. Since the best and brightest of Euro-western society put forth these new theories about the origin of humans, this offered a sense of validity to the policy makers.

Today most Euro-western scholars would not accept that Indigenous peoples are biologically inferior. However, the idea of inferiority has not fully disappeared. This is especially clear in discussions about Indigenous peoples and culture. Even today there are political parties that advocate equality as long as the equality is based on Euro-western cultural ideals and beliefs. What is not mentioned is that early Euro-western developed governments used this same notion of equality to remove Indigenous peoples from their lands and making them dependent. By preventing Indigenous peoples from benefiting from the wealth that came from those lands, they created the economic situation that many Indigenous peoples are in today – a situation of dependency. In the 1920's, Indian Affairs Minister Duncan Campbell Scott, while dismantling Indigenous cultures and institutions through the residential school system and enfranchisement policies, as well as making it impossible for Indigenous peoples to become self-sufficient, stated the following:

> I want to get rid of the Indian problem. I do not think it is a matter of fact that this country ought to continuously protect a class of people, who are able to stand alone. That is the whole point. I do not want to pass into citizens a class of people who are paupers. This is not the intention of the Bill. But after one hundred years, after being in close contact with civilization it is enervating to the individual or a band to continue in that state of tutelage, when he or they are able to take their positions as British citizens or Canadian citizens. To support themselves and stand alone.

That has been the purpose of Indian Education and advancement since the earliest of times. One of the very earliest enactments was to provide for the enfranchisement of the Indians. So it is written in our law that the Indian was eventually to become enfranchised. Our objective is to continue until there is not a single Indian in Canada that has not been absorbed into the body politic and there is no Indian question, and no Indian department, that is the whole objective of this Bill. (Titley p. 50)

Indigenous knowledge systems have endured the brunt of such policies. Ironically, it has been maintained that it is Indigenous culture, not government policy that hold Indigenous people back. What this situation does is take responsibility away from those who have created the conditions that Indigenous peoples endure. As well, it establishes in the minds of the dominant society that Indigenous people have little to offer in terms of knowledge to the world.

The rest of this book are included some of the historical encounters between Newcomers and Indigenous peoples that have led to the present situation. An emphasis will be placed on those encounters in what is now called Canada. However, we have look to the initial encounters to better understand how we ended up in the place we are in today.

Learning Activity

1. Describe a period in your life when things seemed to be going in a certain direction and then suddenly your whole world changed?

2. Go to the library and find an Indigenous origin story or ask an elder to tell you an origin story?

3. Research the current day policies of the different federal political parties towards Indigenous peoples. How do these policies differ from those advocated by Duncan Campbell Scott in the 1920's?

4. Think for a few minutes about various ecological disasters caused by humans that have occurred during the last few years. List as many as you can? Upon reflection, how might traditional environmental approaches averted or at least minimized these disasters?

Review

1. What are the main motivating factors in Western origin stories and Indigenous origin stories?

2. Note down some of the areas wherein Indigenous origin stories are similar to Western origin stories?

3. How have government policies been influenced by the scientific theories of the nineteenth century?

4. In what ways do you think Indigenous origin stories can be of help in maintaining our world?

References

Banai. Eddy Benton. (1979). The Mishomis Book: *The Ojibway creation story*: Chapter 1 St. Paul, MN: Red School House

Beauchamp, W.M. (1892). The Iroquois trail or footprints of the Six Nations. New York: Arms Press

Berkofer, Robert/1979). The Whiteman's Indian: Images of the American Indian from Columbus to the present. New York: Vintage Books

Hernderson, Sa'kej James. (1992). *Algonquin spirituality: Balancing the opposite.* Mi'kmaq studies 260 at University College of Cape Breton Summer Institute (SIS-011) at California Institute of Integral Studies.

Jennings, Francis. (1976). The Invasion of America. New York: Norton

Johnson, Basil. (1978). Ojibwa heritage

Toronto, ON: McLelland and Stewart

Radin, Paul. (1971). The Trickster: *A study in American Indian mythology.* New York: Schocken Books.

Ross, Allen. (1989). Mitakuye Oyasin. Denver Co: Bear Press

Titley, Brian. (1986). A Narrow Vision Vancouver: UBC Press

FIRST ENCOUNTER: COLUMBUS AND THE TAINO

Introduction

In this first section of encounters, we will look at one of the first recorded meetings that occurred between Indigenous peoples and Europeans (the accounts of the Norse being the first). This is the encounter between Christopher Columbus, an explorer from Castile who sailed on behalf of Spain, and the *Taino* Good Persons and *Kalinga* peoples of what are now the Caribbean Islands. I have chosen to utilize a narrative approach in this section by using the journals of the primary participants during this time, most notably the journals of Christopher Columbus and his adopted *Taino* son, Diego. The purpose behind this section is to dispel some of the myths about Columbus and to offer a more broad understanding of his character. It will also look at the motives of the Spanish Crown and the involvement of the Catholic Church and their relationship with the Indigenous people they encountered. The preliminary will provide information about perceptions that the Spanish had about the people they collectively called Indians, and how that played into their treatment of the people they encountered. This first encounter will set the stage for all other encounters between Indigenous peoples in the Americas in what to them was an old world, and for European peoples a new world to be discovered.

Preliminary

The encounter between Columbus and the Indigenous people named *Taino* in what is now called the Caribbean Islands would be one of the greatest events to occur in the world. It would result in changes to the lives of the Indigenous inhabitants of the Americas and to Europeans. The Indigenous peoples of the Americas would be referred to as Indians, some say because Columbus thought he had landed in India. This theory might be partially true in that the region around Cathay (China) during the fifteenth century was referred to as the Indies. Another theory some have put forward is that Columbus described the Indigenous peoples he met as being *in-dios* or People of God. This was because they were peaceful and lived in what appeared to be a paradise, like the Garden of Eden.

Europe, had been suffering years of decline due to warfare and disease and would prosper from the discovery like it never had before increasing its population tenfold. For the Indians in the Caribbean Islands and the rest of the Americas, whole civilizations would cease to exist, others would be displaced from their homelands, and new societies would replace them. The plagues that had affected Europe for so long would decimate the Indigenous populations of the Americas, resulting in the deaths of 90% of their people. Henry F. Dobbins gives a mortality rate as high as 90–112 million Indigenous people (Jennings p. 30). For the European peoples it would be a new world found, and for the Indigenous peoples an old world lost.

During the first 50 years of the first encounter, between 1492 and 1537, debates would take place in Europe as to whether the new people of the Americas were human beings that had souls. This changed when Pope Paul the III issued a papal bull stating that the Indians were true human beings with souls. The time period in between would result in the justification of the slaughter of thousands, while some scholars say in the millions. That was because prior to Pope Paul's declaration, the Indigenous people would be considered closer to the animal kingdom and as a result were hunted down. Previously, Pope Alexander V1 had already divided up the new lands between Portugal and Spain, rationalizing this by claiming to be the supreme authority over the lands of both Christians and Pagans. He viewed himself as Christ's representative on earth; therefore, the sole authority over all lands in the world. Once the Indians had been declared human beings by Pope Paul, in return for having to forfeit their lands to the Spanish, the Indians would receive the gift of Christianity. The vehicle for this royal decree was the *Requerimiento* which was read to the Indians insisting that they pledge their allegiance to the Pope and Spanish Crown or war would be waged against them. During this time, questions were raised such as:

1) How should the faith be preached to the Indians?
2) Under what conditions could they work for the Spanish?
3) When could war be waged against them?
4) Had the new found world been discovered or conquered? (Sinclair.1992. Ideas).

These became referred to as the 'Just Causes of War' under Christendom and exist in the doctrines of the Catholic Church and some Protestant denominations to this day. As the Spanish began moving from the Caribbean Islands into Mexico, South America and North America, some of the greatest barbarities the world had ever witnessed were taking place. Bartolomé Des Las Casas, a slaveholder and convert to the Christian Dominican order and the first defender of the rights of Indian peoples to their lands, would go on to write:

> "In this time the greatest out rages and slaughtering of people were perpetrated, whole villages depopulated. The Indians saw that without any offense on their part they were despoiled of their lives wives and homes. As they saw themselves perishing by the cruel and inhuman treatment of the Spaniards, crushed to the earth by the horses, cut in pieces by swords, eaten and torn by dogs, many buried alive, and suffering all kinds of exquisite tortures." (Sale p. 159).

While he was Bishop of Chiapas, Mexico, he estimated that around 25 million people were put to death by the Spanish over a forty year period with possibly 3 million deaths in the Caribbean alone. Over time, our international legal system would evolve from these first encounters between Europeans and Indians. Legal dictums were applied, such as *Terra Nullius* or land empty of people, meaning the lack of recognition that there were any worthy people living in the Americas before Columbus. The Doctrine of Discovery, based on the belief of supreme authority of Christians over Pagans and then later, Europeans over Indians and their lands, would undermine the rights of Indigenous peoples. This would last to the present day.

The *encomiènda* system developed by the Spanish would be the precursor of the later reserve and reservation systems in both Canada and the United States. Eventually, other Indigenous groups in other parts of the world would be forced into the same system by Colonial governments. Even the designation of being referred to as an American or Canadian would transfer from the Indigenous peoples of North America to the newly arrived settlers.

Both Manifest Destiny 1845 in the United States, and the 1876 Indian Act in Canada, would eventually become the legal and political foundation in law for the relationship between the Indigenous peoples in both countries. The first states that it was the destiny of Christian Americans to usurp the lands from its Indigenous inhabitants, and the second states that they were incapable of handling their affairs and needed special legislation in order to look after their interests. Both policies and subsequent acts would result in dispossession, poverty and dependency. But first, let us look at what occurred during this first encounter between Christopher Columbus and the *Taino* and *Carib* peoples of the Caribbean by reading the journals of Columbus and Diego. I open this section with Columbus sailing to the so called New World.

Christopher Columbus: A Villain or a Hero?
Christian Spain 1492

Narrator: In August 1492 Christopher Columbus set sail to the New World in three ships.

Columbus sets sail

Many of Columbus's crew were sailors while others like Bartolomé de Torres were murderers and given pardon if they sailed. On October 12th, 1492, the land which Columbus named San Salvador was spotted. There he first encountered the Indigenous peoples from *Guanahani*, and for the next ninety-six days would explore, and then name, the islands and the Indigenous peoples. On each Island he would leave a cross standing to show Christian possession. His men would kneel down in front of the cross which Columbus claims was done in front of the Indigenous people.

Diego Colon *Guaikan* The Remora Fish: "More than thirty young men, most older than me, followed me down to the shore. Gaining height on a dune, I could see the giant gulls were actually huge sails, with men climbed on top of long poles, while others pulled on long ropes from below. I said to my friends "they are something like people." After an hour we saw three boats emerge getting closer and closer. I watched the admiral directly as his eyes scanned the beach from the boat as he saw us. Immediately two men went to assist him but he ignored them, jumping to the dry sand." (Barreiro p. 48).

Columbus first wrote of the people he saw: "They all go around naked as their mothers bore them; and also the women, although I didn't see more than one really young girl. All that I saw were young people, none of them more than 30 years old. They were well built, with very handsome bodies and very good faces; their hair over their eyebrows, except for a little in the back that they wear long and never cut. Some of them paint themselves black and some paint themselves white and some red and some with what they find. And some paint their faces and some of them their whole body and some the eyes only and some only the nose." (Cohen p. 55)

***Guaikan*:** "We were stupefied, eyes wide like sea shells. How does one greet such beings? *Cibanakan*, my father - uncle, responded, "Perhaps the sky. Perhaps they have arrived from the sky. The spirit men of the sky have arrived." He said to the others, "Tell your communities to bring them food and other gifts. . . We must go and tell our elders. They have instructions for such a day. Where these men come from there is no death. We may be lucky today." (Barreiro p. 49)

Narrator: Columbus writes of his intentions for the Indians.

Columbus: "It appears that these people are very poor in everything and worse still they have no iron. In order that they might be friendly to us, I knew that they would be better free and converted to the holy faith by love than force. I gave the Natives some red caps and glass beads which they took so much pleasure and became so much our friends. They bare no arms, nor are they acquainted with them for I showed them my swords and they grasped at them by the blade and cut themselves." (Cohen p. 55)

Columbus continues: "They ought to be good servants and of good intelligence. . . I believe that they would easily make good Christians because it seemed they had no religion. Our lord pleasing I will carry off six of them at my departure to your Highness in order that they may learn to speak." (p.56)

Guaikan: "That night we had a meeting at old *Guanahani* village. The old man title holder of *Guanahani*, *Guanahabax*, chose the opening song. It told of the spiritual twins - our spirit forebears who traveled the clouds, enduring adventures and creating the sea and islands of the world." (Barreiro p. 51)

Cibanakan: *Cibanakan* stood, "I will start to tell of the wondrous day we had. A *Guamiquana* Holy Person has come in three vessels full of hair faced beings. Nothing I have seen prepares us for this day. Yet I saw them smile, mostly. They traded gifts with us, and everything they have is wonderful, just wonderfully wonderful. Small rattles, made of guanine. A cloth so smooth I wanted to eat it. A long sharp edge so sharp and heavy, my cousin *Turey* was cut in his hand as he tried to hold it. (Barreiro p. 51)

Guaikan: I was asked to speak, an honor for some one so young at fifteen. . . . I love the new people. They are of the Sky and of the earth too. They have wonderful things, and as my father relates they think of fire and a flame erupts." (Barreiro p. 52)

Guaikan continues: The next day Columbus captured six of our *Guanahani* people as they left our shores the next morning. I had one of the Spanish boys Rodrigo hide me on the ship. No one else can blame for my capture as I captured myself that day. . . It was the last free day of my life." (Barreiro p. 56)

Narrator: Columbus's attitude would soon turn to the worst as he captured more and more of the Indigenous people.

Columbus: "They are the best people in the world and above all the gentlest. They became so much our friends that it was a marvel. I sent the boats ashore for water and they willingly showed my people where the water was and they themselves carried the full barrels to the boat, and took great delight in pleasing us. They are very gentle and without knowledge of what is evil; nor do they murder or steal. Your highnesses may believe that in all the world there can be no better or gentler people . . . for neither better people nor land can there be . . . All the people show the most singular loving behavior and they speak pleasantly. I assure your Highnesses that I believe that in all the world there is no better people or better country. They love their neighbors as themselves, and they have the sweetest talk in the world, and are gentle and always laughing. They even took pieces of the broken hoops of the wine casks and like beasts gave what they had." (Sale p.100)

The Next Island

Narrator: Columbus had seen that the *Taino* wore little gold pendants in their noses. With his captives Columbus set sail to the next island where he believed his Indigenous captives told him there was more gold.

Guaikan: "We sailed into Cuban waters as we knew *Cubanakan* the *Cacique* Chief who lived at the center of the island of Cuba. Columbus thought *Cubanakan* was the Great Khan, chief of the Mongol People of China. After seeing the few Indians that pulled up in their canoes, Columbus would yell *caona caona* (gold gold). But the *Lacayo Taino* offered no *caona*, only nets, food, fresh water and fruit. We walked for two days and arrived at *Baigua's* village and *Baigua* greeted us with courtesy, in the open *Taino* style." (Barreiro p. 67)

Columbus: "That by means of devout religious persons knowing their language well all would soon become Christians: and thus I hope in our lord that Your highness will appoint such persons with great diligence in order to turn to the Church such great peoples, and that they will convert them, even as they have destroyed those who would not confess the father, the son and the holy spirit: and after their days, as we are all mortal, they will leave their realms in a very tranquil condition and freed from the heresy and wickedness, and will be well received before the eternal creator, whom may it please to give them a long life and a great increase of larger realms and dominions, and the will and disposition to spread the holy Christian religion, as they have done up to the present time, amen. Today, I will launch the ship and make haste to start on Thursday, in the name of God, to go to the south east and seek gold and spices, and discover land." (Duun & Oliver p.141)

Guaikan: We sailed east from there and the ships took in sixteen more *Taino* to be held as captives. This new action disconcerted me. Like our own *Guanahani* people the Cuban *Taino* were selected for their strength and attractiveness. We stopped at one point where we met an old man who held the title of *Guamax* Holy Man. By that time he had heard about the captives in the ship. He spoke to Columbus. (Barriero p. 71)

Guamax: "Here I am in the water, a fish in my river. Understand that my words are clean, like my body in this river. Now hear me, my sons and daughters you have in your canoe. I know they have been swallowed. You are to let them go. Those are my children who belong to me. Now you must respond. Do not take them, for I will curse your red hairs. You will be crazy among the trees and rocks and die a fool." (Barriero p. 72)

Narrator: After two months of sailing Columbus still found no gold and when the Natives saw how happy Columbus became from the few trinkets of gold they gave him they told him to go in land. It would be a few years later that Columbus would find out that there was no truth to the matter.

Columbus then decided to set up a colony with the slave labour of the Taino. One could say it was the birth of European colonization in the New World of the Europeans but an end to the Old World for the Taino.

Columbus: "Nothing was lacking but to know the language and to give them orders, because all that they are ordered to do they will do without opposition."(Sale p. 113)

Espanola

He named the last Island Espanola (Haiti and Dominican Republic). The local chief *Guacanagari* wanted to meet Columbus and sent him gifts of gold.

Columbus spoke of *Guacanagari*: "But for going naked he could be a king anywhere in the world." (Barriero p. 108)

Narrator: Columbus invited these people to join him on ship and over a thousand of these people came on to his ship. It was Christmas Eve.

Guaikan: That night I had a running argument with another *Taino* named *Carey* about the spirituality of Columbus as I had become a main spokesman as we traveled.

Carey: "I have seen them cut themselves. They need water, same as us; they eat like humans, they piss and they drop their leavings. They need their sleep. Most of all they lie with our women." (Barreiro p. 110)

Guaikan: "A god can lie with living women. . ." (p. 110)

Carey: "Guaikan you are hard headed for them!" (p. 110)

Guaikan: Through *Guacanagari* and using me as an interpreter the *Taino* offered young women of various *bohios* Houses in marriage to the Spanish, but the Spanish scoffed at the idea. The old councilors of *Guacanagari* were quicker then me. They did not mind the couplings of hospitality, but got suspicious when not one offer of marriage was accepted.

That night Columbus's ship the Santa Maria hit a reef and began to take water. He sent some of his men to get *Gaucanagari's* help. The chief sent all of the people of the town to help. His own family personally guarded Columbus's valuables as they were being loaded off the ship. Columbus gave orders for his men to build a tower and fortress as well as a moat and named his colony La Navidad. (Barreiro p. 111)

Guaikan: We could understand that the Spanish were intent on obtaining gold, but we wondered why they were so very absorbed in its quest. Why, when just a little gold is a great treasure to be cherished in ceremony? Why, when the earth and the sky and the sea provide so well for our people? Why, when it is only in the sharing of the bounties that we learn not to fight, that we learn to do our tasks together and appreciate how lucky we are to breathe the same air and feel the same heat? (Barreiro p. 112)

Narrator: Columbus hearing that his other ship *The Pinta* had landed on the other side of the island had decided it was time to get back to Castile, Spain. Pinzon, the captain of the ship had found the gold mines and they departed back to Spain with thirty-one captive *Tainos*.

Columbus's Second Voyage

Narrator: Plans were set for a second voyage. Pope Alexander VI issued a papal bull confirming Spanish ownership of all lands discovered by Columbus. Columbus was made an admiral and viceroy and governor of the islands and mainland he had discovered. Of course from the perspective of the Taino, he had discovered nothing as they had lived there for thousands of years.

At the first sighting of land, Columbus put in his diary that the people who inhabited these islands Dominica were *Canabilli* whom Columbus said ate human flesh and were dreaded by the *Taino*.

Guaikan: We anchored in a small cove. *Hojeda*, a Spanish soldier made several forays. He brought back baskets full of bones. He showed them to the admiral, who yelled, "man eaters!" Dr. Chanca found scrapes and notches on the bones and declared them to be tooth marks. On another occasion human bones were also found boiling in a pot. I remarked to the admiral that the boiling and preservation of bones in baskets was more a funerary practice than it was about man-eating, as these were both a custom of our own *Taino* people as well, and we certainly were not man-eaters. We dried our dead in the sun and the rain, then used shell tools to scrape the remaining flesh from the bones. The flesh is buried near where the belly button of the person was originally buried and the bones are either buried, or accommodated in baskets which are kept in the *bohios* of the families. These things are considered sacred among our people. (Barreiro pp.143–144)

Columbus: "You are wrong," the Admiral snapped. "*Guacanagari* told me about these people. And your women cried about them, and your uncle *Cibanakan* commented on their raids." (p.144)

Guaikan: I always felt that these were mostly old stories and beliefs of our people. I have seen a canoe of *Ciquayo* warriors who paddled back from a fight with an enemy's thigh hanging at the bow of the canoe. At special times these men who had been in a fight would taste of the jerky from the thigh bone, at once honoring the warrior and consuming his flesh, spiritually defeating him. What I never heard of was anyone cooking up human meat as a daily food, as basic meals for their people and children. The Spanish began to tell stories of how the man-eaters would castrate their own boys and fatten them up for a barbecue. (p.144)

Narrator: There is no evidence that the Caribs were cannibals. Father Breton, a French priest who lived among the *Carib* wrote in the mid-seventeenth century, "I would complain much more readily of their gentleness toward me." (Sale p. 132)

The First Battle

Narrator: The first battle took place when Columbus chased a canoe of *Caribs*. One of the captured Natives was hauled over the bulwarks of the boat and had his head cut off.

Guaikan: "Watch the man-eater swim now," I remember the priest, Father Buil yells. Cuneo, a Spanish sailor, captured a woman warrior. She was tied down, ". . . better than a mare boys!" he said. "Much better!". *Carey* and I hated him. In a fortnight Cuneo was offering his women captives out for lease at one hundred *marivedies* a session. *Carey* told him, "The woman is brave. Allow her to recover and not be used by so many men." Cuneo delivered a blow to *Carey*'s face and put a knife to his throat, "Don't ever question me dog," he said. "Or I will sell you to these men. You might be better than a mare yourself." (Barriero p.149)

Columbus: "More than twenty of the female captives were taken with their own consent and other women native of the island were surprised and carried off by us. Several of the boys, who were captives, came to us fleeing from the Natives of the island who had taken them prisoner." (Cohen p.135)

Narrator: Columbus's fleet now had a number of captives. This was the first organized transaction of slavery on the part of Columbus. As his journal tells what happened.

Columbus: An announcement was made that whoever wanted them could take as many as he pleased, and when everybody had been supplied there were some four hundred left to escape. Some of them left their babies as they fled. Cuneo, a Spanish sailor reported that about 200 of the captured Indians died and they were cast over the ship. (p.138)

The Colony of La Navidad

When Columbus arrived back at La Navidad his first colonial settlement he found a scene of devastation. The entire forty man garrison had been killed.

Coma, a Spaniard: It had resulted because, "Bad feelings arose and broke out into warfare because of the licentious conduct of our men towards the Indian women, for each Spaniard had five women to minister to his pleasure and the husbands and relatives banded together to avenge this insult." (Sale p.139)

Gaucanagari's **sub chief** *Guababo*: "A ceremony was established to feed our guests. Among our food suppliers were a mother and daughter. The soldier Gutierrez took both women and had his men hold them. Pointing to the women he said, "You are mine." That done, the women cried out and all the *Guaxeri* ran for home. The husband and his brother went to Gutierrez and demanded his wife and daughter back. Without speaking Gutierrez stabbed him. Another Spanish soldier cut his brother. The brother ran, but our *Guaxeri* husband dropped and bled and died. The men hoarded three or four even five women each. Husbands and brothers who demanded their families back were cut and stabbed at will in the weeks that followed, and the people were angered. *Guacanigari* argued with the cacique, *Caonabo* not to take revenge. *Caonabo* fighters took down the Spanish soldiers. By ones and twos, arrows they shot into them and from trees they clubbed them until there were none left." (Barreiro p.153)

Guaikan: As we entered La Navidad, bodies were found but no gold. "Damned Barbarians!" was a favorite expression heard that day. I remember Father Buil was maniacal "They should hang for killing Christians, they should burn!" he demanded. (Barreiro p.155)

Narrator: It was during these first encounters of rape that the myth of the promiscuous Native girl was born in Spain.

The Settlement of Isabella

Narrator: Columbus next set up the colony of Isabella where the killing of Taino became so rampant that some even believed it to be it to be haunted.

Spanish report of Isabella hauntings: Reports circulated about the horrible voices and frightening cries that could be heard day and night by anyone who passed by the town. There was a story about a man walking through the deserted town and coming upon people lining the streets on both sides who were dressed like the best Spanish courtiers. The man, awed by this unexpected vision, greeted them and asked where they came from. But they kept silent, answering only by lifting a hand to their hats as a sign of greeting, and as they took off their hats, the whole head came off so that two files of beheaded gentlemen were left lining the street before they vanished altogether. (Sale p. 143)

Columbus then sent out expeditions in search of gold and when some of his men mutinied. Even after becoming sick the Spanish wouldn't eat the many nourishing vegetables found on the island, believing they were the food of the devil. For the next six years until 1500, Columbus remained at Isabela on the island of Espanola. While Columbus was off on a voyage to Cuba he made the islands into a Catholic Sovereign.

Fernando his son reported: "Each one went where he willed among the Indians stealing their property and wives and inflicting so many injuries upon them that the Indians resolved to avenge themselves." (Sale p.153)

Narrator: The *Taino* despised the Spanish and when Columbus returned he assembled an army to capture or destroy the Natives in the valley of Vega Real. There they came across a large number of *Taino* slaughtering them with their superior guns and swords. Columbus had noses and ears chopped off of *Taino* who didn't understand the Spanish concept of property. Every *Taino* over the age of fourteen had to supply the rulers with a hawk's bell full of gold every three months. If they didn't, they had their hands cut off. (Sale p.155)

Xarague *the Last Free Taino State*

Guaikan: *Xarague* was the last free *Taino* state. *Bohekio* its old cacique Chief had died and was replaced by his sister *Anacaona*. When the Spanish entered *Anacaona* told me to tell the Spanish that she wanted peace. The visit began with song and ceremony and with a feast and dance. Some eighty caciques gathered to celebrate. Commander Ovando was an austere man of the church. *Anacaona* sat next to Ovando and I could tell her diplomacy bothered him. That night I heard him say late in the evening "A rebellion is in the offing. The filthy slut won't let things be. She is in need of a Christian example." The next day he told her that he would have a mass performed for all of her *caciques*. They were brought into one of the large huts. Suddenly Valazquez seized *Anacaona*, looped a rope around her wrists and brought her out. She cried to him, "What have we done to you?" He replied, "You are soiled as a mud snake. By authority of the Church and king, I will hang you for your sins against nature." Holding lances and swords at the ready the *caciques* were tied up and threatened that if they didn't renounce Anacaona they would be roasted. "Fire to the devils", Valazquez cried out! All around the hut was lit and a fire roared in minutes. Seeing what happened, the *Guaxeri* fought well. They attacked fearlessly trying to get to their burning *caciques*. Indians not captured had retreated into the forest while captives were crammed into *bohios* and threatened with death. (Barreiro p. 240–241)

Encomienda

Narrator: Columbus installed the encomiènda system which stated that any Spanish person could make an Indigenous person his personal slave on the condition that he is made a Christian in return. The policy was made official on Espanola in 1502, sanctioned by the crown in 1503, and would be in effect when the Spanish invaded Mexico, Peru and Florida. It would be the precursor to the reserve/reservation system that would be set up in North America. The African slave trade would also start in 1505 as the Native people were killed off.

Narrator: Bartolomé Des Las Casas arrived in 1502, himself an encomendero, or slave owner, before taking his religious vows.

Las Casas: "The Spanish made bets as to who could slit a man in two, or cut off his head at one blow or they opened up his bowels. They tore the babies from their mother's breasts by their feet and bashed them against rocks. They spitted the bodies of other babies together with their mothers and all who were before them on their swords." (Sale p.157).

Narrator: By 1542 Las Casas writes that there were only 200 *Taino* left (p. 161). Today there are none in existence and very few other Indigenous people in the Caribbean. In 1500 Francisco Bobadilla replaced Columbus. In spite of the fact that thousands of *Taino* had been murdered by Columbus and none remain today, he was never charged with one of their deaths.

Learning Activity

1. Have several students read out the different parts in the text in front of the class: The Narrator; Columbus; and *Guaikan*.

2. Ask the class what they feel and think about what has just been read. Does the material coincide with what they had already learned in school?

3. Ask the class to look up the living conditions in Europe and in the Americas before 1492.

4. Today, who are the people who live in the Caribbean Islands? How did they get there?

Review

1. When Columbus and *Diego Guaikan* met one another, what do you think their impressions of each other were?

2. How do you think the relationship between Columbus and the *Taino* could have been better?

3. Why do you think that Columbus might be looked upon as a villain by Indigenous people and a hero by others in North America?

4. What is do you think the difference is between a conquest and a discovery?

References

Barriero, Jose. (1993). The Indian chronicles. Huston: Arte Público Press

Sinclair, Lister. The Just Causes of War In *Ideas*. Canada: C.B.C. Radio (1992/01/03).

Jennings, Francis. (1976). *The invasion of America: Indians, colonialism and the cant of conquest.* New York, London: W.W. Norton Company.

Sale, Kirkpatrick. (1990). The conquest of paradise. New York: Plume.

Cohen, J.M. (Ed.). (1969). *The four voyages of Christopher Columbus: being his own log – book, letters, and dispatches with connective narrative drawn from the life of the Admiral by his son Hernando Colon and other contemporary historians*. Harmondsworth, Middlesex: Penguin Books.

Dunn, Oliver and Kelly & James Jr. (1989). The Diary of Coumbus's First voyages. *Abtsract from Fray Bartolomé De Las Casas*. Oklahoma Press

ENCOUNTERS BETWEEN INDIGENOUS PEOPLES AND NEWCOMERS IN EASTERN NORTH AMERICA: REMEMBERING THE BEOTHUK OF NEWFOUNDLAND

Introduction

When we read about Indigenous and Newcomer relations in Canadian History, we sometimes make comparisons between the way Indigenous peoples were treated in the United States and in Canada. The Indigenous experience in the United States seemed much more adversarial than in Canada, and on the whole it was. However, this isn't to say that the history of Canada as it evolved into a nation was always a result of compromise between French, English and Indigenous peoples.

In New France, except for conflicts with the *Rotinonshonni* (Iroquois), relations remained pretty stable between Indigenous peoples and the French. After the conquest of New France by the English in 1760, things would change, and Indigenous peoples would face their most difficult times ahead. However, even before 1760, tenuous relations between English settlers in the last province to join Canadian Confederation, Newfoundland, and an Indigenous people who lived there, resulted in a genocide taking place. The people involved were the *Beothuk*.

In order to understand why this happened we must remember that from the very beginning there had been continuous conflict between Indigenous peoples and the English on the eastern coast of North America. The fall of New France in 1760 to the English, had brought the first influx of English settlers into British North America. After the American Revolutionary War of 1776 and the War of 1812, mass migration of English Loyalist settlers from the United States would change the demographics of British North America and then Canada forever. With their arrival, they also brought with them the same attitudes towards Indigenous peoples as their American counterparts, but without the means and military might to achieve a victory over them. Instead of using military force they would try to first divide Indigenous nations into small sub groups, restrict them to small plots of land and then legislate them out of existence (see chapter five). In the case of the *Beothuk*, they would face the same situation as other Indigenous groups along the East Coast of North America; extinction. This section will touch on the early period of English and Indigenous relations with an emphasis on the *Beothuk* people who once inhabited the island of Newfoundland.

Preliminary

Throughout the 16th and 17th century, Europe was filled with religious strife. As some Christians began to protest abuses occurring within the Catholic Church, they began to break away, creating their own Christian denominations. They would be referred to as Protestants because they protested the abuses of power by the Catholic Church. These Protesters or Protestants would be the catalysts for mass emigration to the North East Coast of the Americas. As the monarchs of Europe gained power and the exclusive right to rule their countries, the result was that the Catholic Church began to lose secular and religious power. Meanwhile, French Catholics in the 17th century were developing trade relationships in the Upper North East of North America. However, there was no incentive to settle en mass in the country they would name Canada from the Iroquoian word *Kanata* Place of My Village; therefore, relations with Indigenous peoples remained amicable.

At the same time in England, history was about to take an ominous turn that would affect the lives of Indigenous peoples on the East Coast of North America. The mid to late half of 16th century England, was ruled by Henry VIII, who, unable to acquire a divorce broke away from the Catholic Church and founded the Church of England. Over the next century, Protestants began to migrate to North America feeling that the Protestant religion practiced in England wasn't strict enough in its teachings and practices. They wanted to practice a more fundamentalist form of Christianity that was more personal, and rigid. Some of these Protestants were referred to as Pilgrims while others were referred to as Puritans. These Pilgrims and Puritans saw North America as a new Israel promised to them in their biblical teachings, and themselves as the chosen people predetermined by God to take over the country. They thought they could build a city modeled after Old Jerusalem in the bible.

Eventually, members of the Church of England would follow the Pilgrims and Puritans, who up until the American Revolutionary War would become the most influential Christian Protestant denomination in British North America. They would later be known as Episcopalians and in Canada, Anglicans. Still others arrived such as the Ana Baptists who were fleeing religious persecution from other Christians in Europe. Still, others arrived for the opportunities that the new land held.

Unfortunately for the Indigenous peoples living in the areas where both the Pilgrims and Puritans landed, they would be perceived much like the Canaanites in the bible of old Israel, to be smitten down by the new chosen people, the Christians, just as the ancient Hebrews had done to the Canaanites (Lippy, Coquette, and Poole, 1992, p. 268). The Pilgrims would land in Massachusetts Bay while the Puritans arrived in what is now Virginia. After finding a place they could practice Christianity the way they wanted, they would then impose their beliefs on the Indigenous peoples by attacking their spirituality as a form of Devil worship. This would last until 1978. The first to feel the brunt of the attacks were the spiritual leaders of the Indigenous communities. They would use Christianity as a justification for making war on the Indigenous peoples and confiscating their land. Similar to the writings of other Puritans at the time, Increase Mather wrote:

> Lord God of our fathers hath given us rightful possession the land of the Heathen People amongst whom we live. . . . That they had remained quite so long must be ascribed to the wonderful providence of God who did lay the fear of the English and the dread of them upon the Indian. The terror of God was upon them round about. There could be no clearer equation: the dread of the English was the terror of God (Jennings; p. 183).

Many years later when the new country called the United States was formed out of the original thirteen English colonies, it would become government policy known as Manifest destiny that would allow for Protestant Christians to continue making war on Indians and taking away their lands and dismantling their cultural beliefs.

Attitudes by Increase Mather and other Protestant colonists towards Indigenous peoples were contradictory and often didn't make much sense. They often wrote that the Indians were uncivilized hunters who didn't know how to till the soil like Christians; therefore, their lands should go to civilized farmers. Civilization, farming and the Protestant religion would become synonymous with one another over the next three centuries. The truth was most Indians in the areas where the Protestants settled were primarily agriculturalists, showing the settlers how to grow new crops like corn, beans, squash, sweet potato, and cranberry. In fact three fifths of crops feeding the world in this present day were first cultivated by Indigenous farmers in the Americas (Weatherford p. 71).

In a few years the Protestants would depopulate most of the East Coast of its Indigenous inhabitants by way of warfare and disease. At around the same time the Puritans had arrived in Virginia around 1609, English Protestants began to settle in a place they would call the New Found Land. Most would arrive because of the abundant stocks of fish rather than for lands to farm. The Indigenous population of this New Found Land would suffer the same fate as other Indigenous peoples along the East Coast. They would cease to exist as a people. The Indigenous people who lived on this island would be known as the *Beothuk*. Who were these people that have come to be named *Beothuk*?

Previous to the arrival of other Europeans, about 1,000 A.D., Norse sailors from Greenland had already settled in the northern part of Newfoundland, in a place that has come to be known as Lance aux Meadows. Norse legends explain that after settling down and at first living in peace with the Indigenous people in the area, they eventually fought with them and were forced to leave. It is possible that during the first contacts between both groups Norse men and *Beothuk* women developed relationships with one another; therefore, the result would have been *Beothuk* children with a lighter pigment of skin as was reported by later explorers. Due to the early demise and lack of contact with the *Beothuk*, we cannot be sure.

The *Beothuk* were probably known by other Indigenous peoples, possibly as far as Hudson's Bay in the north. Cree elder and historian, Louis Bird, believes that they were possibly descended from a people they referred to as *Puatuk* who predated the arrival of the Thule people (Inuit) and migrated from the Hudson's Bay region east (Louis Bird, 2001, Personal Correspondence). These have become known by archeologists as the Dorset people. The Cree word *Puatuk* was a common term used in various Algonquin languages with differing pronunciations that signified enemy. It is possible that the name *Beothuk* was given to explorers by another Indigenous people they were in conflict with and their name isn't *Beothuk* at all but something completely different. We know from some historical sources that the *Beothuk* and *Mi'kmaq* didn't always get along.

It is almost a certainty that Basque fishermen would have encountered the *Beothuk* during their long fishing voyages, as Basque whaling stations have been found along the Saint Lawrence River that date back to the fifteenth century and before.

In the year 1499, explorer John Cabot was said to have brought three captives back with him to England. Upon arriving in England, and in fear of losing the rights to this newly discovered land, Spain made a claim to it based on Columbus's discovery of the Indies which had been given to Spain by Pope Alexander VI in 1492. Upon exploration by Corte Real, Portugal also attempted to claim this New Found Land as their own, calling it 'Terra de Baccalaos' or Land of the Cod. (Marshall p. 15) Even France became involved by putting a small settlement on the island, although it wouldn't last long. Therefore, at one time most of the powerful European trading nations claimed the New Found Land as their own at one time.

How long had the *Beothuk* lived on the island? No one can be sure. It is from the *Beothuk* that the moniker given to all Indigenous peoples in the Americas, 'red Indian' and then the more derogatory expression 'red skin' was first derived. The name came into significance after John Cabot's second voyage in 1498, as a way to describe the use of red ochre pigment on their bodies. Like many other Indigenous peoples, the *Beothuk* utilized red ochre in both their ceremonies and burials. They mined red ochre pigment at a place now called Conception Bay. By September 14, 1829, some 42 years before Canada would become a country, the entire *Beothuk* culture would pass out of existence. They would face the same fate as many of the other Indigenous societies on the East Coast and that was extinction as a people. The question may be asked, "How did it happen?"

The Demise of the *Beothuk* Peoples of Newfoundland

We find from early encounters, that the relationship between the newcomers and the *Beothuk* was a tenuous one from the very beginning. It would become more so with the arrival of the English. Our first description of them comes from Corté Real who captured fifty of them. However it was Alberto Cantino and Pietro

Pasqualigo who would first describe the *Beothuk* as looking like gypsies and were said to be tall with long black hair and of gentile disposition and given to laughter. (Marshall pp. 16–17)

We know by the writings of Cabot, Real and others, that the *Beothuk* were a healthy and robust people. Some *Beothuk* were even reported to be gigantic in stature. We must remember during this period of time, the average European male was about five feet three inches tall, partly due to an insufficient diet in Europe. A *Beothuk* measuring six feet, a common height for a healthy man today, would have appeared to be very large in height and maybe even gigantic. It is also well to be remembered that European explorers exaggerated some of their stories about their travels when they arrived back in Europe sometimes telling tales of monstrous looking people and beasts. This often placed Indigenous peoples in difficult situations with the newcomers. It was during this time that Indigenous peoples of the newly discovered world were the subject of debates in Europe, as to whether they were human beings and had souls (see chapter one). Therefore, there wasn't any regulation in place against killing them. For the *Beothuk* this concept would continue long after Indigenous peoples were declared human beings.

The Beothuk People

What we do know about the *Beothuk* is that they were probably members of the Algonquin language family. This means that most of the people who inhabited the region spoke a similar, but not the same, language as other groups in the region. There are similar words found among the *Beothuk* and other Algonquin peoples. We know this because an Englishman named William Cormack wrote down some of the *Beothuk* language and these few words are our only link to the *Beothuk* language.

From the writings of *Shawnadithit*, the last *Beothuk* to survive, we know the *Beothuk* practiced the sweat lodge and possibly a tradition known as the vision quest. This is a ceremony in which a young boy and sometimes girl, about the age of twelve, goes alone into the woods for a period of four days without food or water and acquires a guardian spirit. The spirit comes by way of a vision the young person has had during the fast. Archeologists who study the bones and burial items of ancient people have found bone pendants of animals in *Beothuk* burial sites that show that they probably acquired guardian spirits for protection (Marshall p. 326). A pendant is similar to a necklace. It usually has an engraving of an animal or something in nature. A young person, upon receiving a guardian spirit such as a bear, would wear the pendant with engraving of the bear. If needed, they could call to the spirit of the bear to help bring them good fortune.

As mentioned, the *Beothuk* utilized the sweat lodge ceremony as well. A sweat lodge is made out of saplings of willow or poplar. It is dome-shaped and consists of eight poles with four placed around in a horizontal position, and four others crossing over. It is then covered with the skins of animals; in the case of the *Beothuk* it would probably have been the skins of the black bear. Within the sweat lodge, stones referred to as grandfathers, because they are the oldest objects in the world, are heated by fire. Some Algonquin societies believe that stones have stored memories of events that go back to the beginning of time. If we look at this concept from a different point of view it is easier to explain. Today, scientists are able to tell how old things are by measuring the carbon sediment that accumulates on rocks and other objects through time and in a sense this is a form of memory. During the sweat lodge ceremony, water is placed on the grandfather rocks heated in a fire. The steam that is formed from the evaporating water then cleanses the person. The sweat lodge is still used by Algonquin peoples. After being captured, the mother of *Shawnadithit* would make a sweat lodge for her other daughter and try to cure her. Unfortunately she did not survive.

During the time the *Beothuk* were still living, the island of Newfoundland had nine species of animals that the *Beothuk* could live off of. The caribou was the most important, followed by the black bear and beaver. They also relied on the food that came from the ocean and rivers for their survival. For a long time they had a well-balanced livelihood. During the summer months they would live near inlets and coves of rivers and the Atlantic Ocean, fishing for salmon. Other times they would hunt seals, porpoises, and whales. In order to travel on water, the *Beothuk* had a unique style of birch bark canoe with sides that rose up to a point and higher than the bow and the stern. This allowed them to travel on the ocean, preventing high waves from entering the sides of the canoe. In this way they were able to travel to places like Fogo Island, where they collected eggs from a bird we call a cormorant.

During the spring and fall months, they fished in lakes, one of which is now referred to as Red Indian Lake. One of the main rivers they canoed is now called the Exploits River. It was along this river that the *Beothuk* made their last stand. During the severe winters, the *Beothuk* would leave the coast and move into the interior to get away from the piercing northerly winds that came off of the ocean. There they would hunt the migrating caribou herds. The best time for the *Beothuk* to hunt would have been when the top snow became crisp, as that is when the hoofs of the caribou would sink in the snow, slowing their movement. Today, moose brought to Newfoundland by hunters at the turn of the twentieth century have replaced the caribou. However, in the past some moose did exist on the island probably drifting over on ice flows.

The *Beothuk* referred to their lodges as *mamateeks*. Some of these were small and portable, meaning they could be carried from place to place. There were others that were larger and could hold as many as fifteen people. When first discovered by the settlers, they were surprised at how well they were built. Moss was used as an insulator between the planks, which were set like a log cabin. The planks were then placed in a conical position towards the top, with an opening to let the smoke from the fire get out. *Shawnadithit* drew pictures of what a *mamateek* looked like. Smaller *mamateeks* were covered with animal and fish skins and used during the summers. This allowed for mobility. Imagine it this way. It is like a family having a large home for the winter and having a smaller camp during the summer where they can go fishing and the kids can go swimming and play. Today, we can see a similar structure to a *mamateek* built by the Cree in the James Bay region as a winter hunting camp. (Marshall pp. 350–360).

In 1612, an English merchant named John Guy set up a trading post in the South East region of New-foundland at Conception Bay and changed the lives of the *Beothuk* for ever (Marshall p. 27). At first trade relations between the English and *Beothuk* remained cordial; especially around Trinity Bay where a trading post had been set up. Henry Crout would follow Guy, by continuing the good trading relations. By 1620 over sixty English ships would be anchored around Trinity Bay. Some of the fishermen believed the Beo-thuk had stolen some of their fishing gear and fired on them resulting in the beginning of bad relations. A second incident occurred in 1639 when the crew of a fishing vessel took a cannon shot at the *Beothuk*. (Marshall p. 38)

One could understand the reluctance of the *Beothuk* to have anything to do with Europeans thereafter. Most of their experiences had been bad, whether it was with the Norse years before, or the Portuguese and then the English.

The firing of the canon would portend the beginning of the end of the relationship between the English and the *Beothuk*. More and more settlers would arrive on the southern part of the island. They forced the *Beothuk* to the northern part of Newfoundland where they became increasingly isolated. There they remained away from danger until settlers arrived in the Exploits Bay region in 1729. The settlers began to take over the summer fishing spots of the *Beothuk*. It resulted in the *Beothuk* being excluded from the much-needed marine life on the coast and the mouth of the rivers. The *Beothuk* were being forced into starvation. Disease from fisherman was starting to affect them as well. In order to survive, during the night the *Beothuk* would try to steal supplies from the fishermen only to be chased further into the interior.

As a result of being forced into the interior by the fishermen the *Beothuk* became more and more depen-dent on the wildlife, which was seasonal. Furthering their loss was the fact that they could no longer hunt and fish the marine life from the ocean, such as the seal, whale and seabirds without being shot at.

Rumours were beginning to trickle south about what was happening in the lawless north of the island. In 1768, the Governor of Newfoundland, Hugh Pallaser, sent a man named John Cartwright to investigate the rumours (Marshall p. 240). He was horrified by what he heard and saw. Fisherman often bragged about how many *Beothuk* they were able to kill. The *Beothuk* were being hunted down like fur-bearing animals.

Besides fisherman, furriers with experience in the woods began to track down the *Beothuk* (Marshall p. 71). These men were as experienced as the *Beothuk* in the woods. Some of the furriers happened to be *Mi'kmaq*. Certainly *Mi'kmaq* furriers like Noel Boss were involved. However, they were few in number and were paid by Englishmen like William Payton to hunt *Beothuk* down. Most of the furriers were Englishmen.

In 1803, William Cull, a furrier was paid fifty pounds (the equivalent of a hundred dollars) for a *Beothuk* woman he had captured. This event set the stage for the final chapter in the *Beothuk* story. The price to hunt *Beothuk* was raised to one hundred pounds by 1810. This was alot of money at the time. During this time there were said to be only seventy-two *Beothuk* left alive. Many had died from gunshot wounds, others from starvation, and still others from disease brought from Europe such as smallpox and measles (Steckley p. 106).

One day, the hated furrier William Cull with fourteen others went into the interior to hunt *Beothuk*. Under the leadership of David Buchan, they surrounded a *Beothuk* woman named *Shawnadithit* and her remaining people. After several hours of negotiations they left two of their men with the *Beothuk* and took four *Beothuk* with them. Buchan himself had privately bragged about killing twenty-nine *Beothuk*. A *Beothuk* man named *Nonobawsuit* was one of the *Beothuk* taken captive. He was *Shawnadithit's* uncle. What happened next is still unclear as we only have the furrier's side of the story. What we do know is that *Nonobawsuit* began to run from the furriers. We do not know what happened to the other three Beothuk. Seeing him running towards them in fear and believing they were under attack by the furriers, the *Beothuk* killed the two furriers with them and then made their escape. They hung the heads of the two men on a pole, perhaps as a warning (Marshall pp. 129–132). This angered the furriers who wanted revenge for the killings. From this time on the remaining *Beothuk* would live a perilous existence.

Over the remaining years of her life, *Shawnadithit* would have other close calls with the furriers. One day, while washing clothes, *Shawnadithit* was hit with buckshot. Some say the culprit was Noel Boss, the feared *Mi'kmaq* furrier.

Of all the Newfoundland settlers who the Beothuk would come to hate, none would surpass John Payton Sr. and his son John Payton Jr. While in a fit of rage, John Payton Sr. had been known to have clubbed to death several *Beothuk*. (Steckley p. 113) In 1819, John Payton Sr., his son, and his men surprised and captured *Shawnadithit's* aunt *Demasduit*. Carrying her baby in her arms she tried to get away. Her strength had been sapped from a recent illness and she was too ill to run. *Nonobawsuit* tried to save her but was shot dead by Payton and his men. After *Demasduit* was captured, she was renamed Mary March for the month of her capture. At the time it had become illegal to capture or kill a *Beothuk*, like an endangered species there was a sense that they needed to be protected. Payton was charged but then released. Damasduit after trying to escape three times was promised that one day she would be returned to her people, but caught tuberculosis and died before she could get back to her village. This may have been a ploy to capture other *Beothuk* (Steckley pp. 117–121).

By 1822, there were only twenty-seven *Beothuk* left, *Shawnadithit*, her mother and sister, were soon captured by the infamous furrier, William Cull who then turned her over to the hated William Payton Jr. (Steckley p. 122) In captivity *Shawnadithit* was renamed Nancy April for the month of her capture and lived the few remaining years as a servant for Payton and others. Her mother and sister would pass on before her. Each day, *Shawnadithit* was reported going into the woods and upon her return claimed she had visited her sister and mother. Perhaps in some strange way we don't understand she had or perhaps she was just lonely for them. It would be because of *Shawnadithit's* drawings that we would learn the few things we know about the *Beothuk* culture. Today some of these drawings still survive and have been documented in various books about them.

In 1829 *Shawnadithit* after living with several different families, finally succumbed to tuberculosis. She was the last of the *Beothuk* that we know existed at the time. Her skull was taken for scientific research and body buried somewhere in St. Johns, Newfoundland (Steckley p. 31). There was a story that went around for a time that fisherman had seen some *Beothuk* canoe out into the ocean towards the coast of Labrador sometime after her death, but we will never know for sure. Still today, some people in Newfoundland claim to have *Beothuk* ancestry. What we do know for certain is that as a people they were never seen again in Newfoundland.

Learning Activity

1. Look up a map of the East Coast of North America. Try and find where James town Virginia and Plymouth Bay are.

2. Look at a map of Newfoundland and find Exploits Bay, Red Indian Lake, Conception Bay and Fogo Island.

3. Read something about the Island of Newfoundland today: demographics and economy.

4. Find out if there are still any Indigenous people on the Island of Newfoundland. Who are they? Where did they come from?

Review

1. What are the names of the Indigenous people mentioned in the text? What does the name of the Indigenous people of Newfoundland mean?

2. Who was *Shawnadithit* and why is she important to the text?

3. Explain some of the things you learned about the culture of the Indigenous people of Newfoundland?

4. What happened to the Indigenous people of Newfoundland?

References

Bird, Louis. (2001). Personal Correspondence. University of Winnipeg.

Jennings, P. (1976). The invasion of America: Indians, Colonialism, and the Cant of Conquest. New York/London: Norton & Company

Lippy, C., Choquette, R. & Poole, S. (1992). Christianity Comes to America. New York: Paragon.

Marshall, Ingeborg. (1996). A History of Ethnography of the Beothuk. Montreal & Kingston: McGill/Queens University Press.

Steckley, John. (2011). Beyond Their Years: *five native women's stories*. Three O'clock Press: Toronto

MORE ENCOUNTERS BETWEEN NEWCOMERS AND INDIGENOUS PEOPLES IN EASTERN CANADA

Introduction

Besides the preliminary that gives a brief description about the Algonquin people of the Ottawa River Valley, this section will describe the traditions and cultures of two Indigenous peoples in the east, the *Mi'kmaq* and *Wendat*. In the text I use the name Algonquin for the people who live along the *Kischisippi* Great River (Ottawa River); however, they refer to themselves as *Anishnaabe* First Human *To Fall To The Earth*, not to be confused with the Ojibwa, Pottowotomie, and Odawa who also refer to themselves as *Anishnaabe* although they are closely related. Their name for themselves is the same as the other three because in the past they were the same group of people who separated into various designations during their great migration from the east to the west. The *Anishnaabe*, *Mi'kmaq*, and *Wendat* were significant in the relationships that were developing between the French and Indigenous peoples in Canada during the seventeenth century.

Preliminary

The Anishnaabe *(Algonquin)*

The French began to establish themselves around the former Indigenous village named *Hochelaga Otsiraga* Place Of The Council Fire, later named Ville Marie in 1643 by the French, and now known as Montreal. From as early as 1603 the French had developed alliances with two Indigenous peoples in the area. They were the *Anishnaabe* First Humans (Algonquin) of the *Kichisippi* Great River (Ottawa River) and the *Wendat* Islanders (Huron) who lived in *Taranto* Where The Fish Weirs Are Set. It was a name given to the area between Georgian Bay and the Trent River basin by the *Wendat*. It would later become the name of the largest city in Canada, Toronto. Along with the *Kaniatarowanenneh* Great River of the Iroquois *Rotinonshonni* Longhouse People (St. Lawrence River), the *Kichisippi* Great River of the *Anishnaabe* (Algonquin) was the main route to the interior.

Both the name Iroquois and Algonquin were names given to the *Rotinonshonni* and *Anishnaabe* by the French. There are various theories as to why the French called the *Rotinonshonni* Longhouse People, Iroquois. One theory is that before entering a village members of the *Rotinonshonni* would cry out three times *quois, quois, quois*. It was a custom that signified a call that they were entering a village to notify the death of someone (Thomas, 1992, Personal Correspondence). Others say it cake from a Basque word describing the people.

We have a better idea as to why the *Anishnaabe* of the *Kichisippi* were called Algonquin. In the year 1603, Samuel de Champlain witnessed a victory dance on the North Shore of *Kaniatarowanenneh* River. It was being held by several groups of Indigenous peoples including the *Mi'kmaq, Malecete* and *Innu*. These people spoke a similar language and lived near the Great Eastern Ocean. There was a third group of people who were doing a victory dance at the time of Champlain's visit. Champlain asked who they were. A *Malicete* chief misunderstood the question and pointed to the people saying *Algolikan*, 'people who are dancing' in his language. Champlain thought it was the name of the people dancing and forever after these people were referred to as Algonquin. (Champlain) From that time on anyone who spoke a similar language as the dancing people was referred to as a speaker of an Algonquian language (Clément p. 1).

The *Anishnaabe* Algonquin, who lived along the *Kichisippi* Great River (Ottawa River), would become very important to the French, because in order for them to trade with the nations west, they would have to pass through their territory. The *Algonquin (Anishnaabe), Malecete, Mi'kmaq* and *Innu* had all battled the *Rotinonshonni* with the *Mi'kmaq* calling them *Kwedesh* Enemy and the *Algonquins* referring to them as *Nadoway* Snakes.

It would be in the territory of the *Anishnaabe* Algonquin where much of the fighting would take place between the *Rotinonshonni* and the Algonquian speaking peoples. This would have devastating consequences for the Algonquin who lived along the *Kichisippi*. Further along the *Kichisippi* was a tributary called the *Mattawa* Meeting Place. Past *Mattawa* and several lakes beyond lived another people who referred to themselves as *Wendat* Islanders. It would be along these river routes that the fur trade would take place opening up the country to Catholic missionaries, traders, and finally settlers.

During the early part of the seventeenth century, the *Rotinonshonni* had blocked off some of the major water ways like the *Kichisippi*, and the French needed them opened up to pass through. An abundance of beaver along the north shore of the river and access to the interior made this waterway of prime importance to the French. They also wanted to develop a trading relationship with the *Wendat*. Some of the tributaries that diverted from the *Kichisippi* led right up to the Great Bay in the North, where Dutch funded explorer Henry Hudson had sailed and where the English wanted to establish themselves. Others rivers led to *Taranto*. If the French could gain passage through the *Kichisippi*, it would put them in a very strategic trading position with the Indigenous peoples in the interior.

In the same year that Champlain had witnessed the dance taking place, Grave Du Pont a French explorer had brought back with him to France several *Innu* The People (Montagnais) where they were treated like royalty. The Beaver Felt hat was the style in France at the time; therefore, they had a desire for the thick furs of the northern beaver. In order to access them, they would need alliances with peoples such as the *Innu, Anishnaabe* (Algonquin) and *Wendat*. It was due to the mercury solution used on the fur which poisoned many of the felt hat manufacturers that resulted in the expression he is as mad as a hatter which became famous in the children's story, Alive in Wonderland.

In exchange for furs the French would trade items such as metal pots and hatchets. Sometimes they would trade liquor as well. This would cause problems for many Indigenous peoples in the future as it had done for so long among Europeans. One of the things the *Anishnaabe, Innu, Wendat* and others sought was the arquebus. This was a proto type of a rifle that was in use at the time. After been attacked by Samuel De Champlain with the help of the *Anishnaabe* and *Wendat*, the *Rotinonshonni* were acquiring the arquebus from the Dutch. It would have devastating consequences for the Indigenousl allies of the French.

The *Rotinonshonni* lived south of the *Algonquians* and had being at war with them for several years referring to them as *Atirondoks* Bark Eaters and those *Anishnaabe* west of them *Tehakunus* Different Speakers. They also had a name for the French and that was *Assaroni* Hatchet Makers because of the knives and hatchets the French traded with the *Algonquians* to use against them.

The *Anishnaabe* (Algonquin) had displaced the brethren of the *Rotinonshonni* who had lived around *Hochelaga* Place Of The Council Fire (Montreal) After defeating them, they adopted some of them among their people. These former *Rotinonshonni* would be headed by a leader the French would call *Iroquet*. *Iroquet* explained how he had once lived on the island years before with his people called *Ononchateronon*. Some of the *Ononchateronon* had moved south to live among their brethren, the *Rotinonshonni,* especially the *Kenienke:haka* Flint People (Mohawk), or had moved west to live among *Wendat*. Others such as *Iroquet* after being captured had become nationalized Algonquin. *Iroquet* would be the one to convince the *Wendat* leader *Ochastequin*, to join him and the French on an expedition against the *Kenienke:haka* in 1609. We are nor sure why he became such an advent enemy of the *Kenienke:haka* (Grassman pp. 13–14).

To this day, the *Kenienke:haka* Flint People (Mohawk) refers to the island of Montreal as *Tiotiake* Where The People Split Apart as they believe they have a historical relationship to this place before leaving it for the first time. Those captives adopted among the victorious *Anishnaabe* such as *Iroquet* became members of the Martin Clan *Wabizhasi Dodem* and would be known for their prowess in war (Benton p. 96). Years later, around the year 1670, after years of fighting with some of their *Kenienke:haka* brethren they would live together in peace once again in the *Kenienke:haka* villages of *Kahnawake* By The Rapids and then later in *Kanehsatake* Where There Are Sandbanks. Both villages would be established across from *Tiotiake* Where The People Split (Montreal). The Algonquins would keep their own name for *Kanehsatake* and call it *Oka* Place Of The Pickerel. Here they would once again commingle and intermarry with one another. However, the *Kenienke:haka* would become the dominant society in the village and *Kenienké:ha* (Mohawk) the dominant language spoken.

What solidified the relationship between the *Anishnaabe* (Algonquin), *Wendat* and the French in trade was the exchange of young people between them. It had been a custom among many Indigenous nations that upon making an alliance with one another, they were to adopt each others young people to live among them as their own. As these young people became integrated into the community, it meant there would be a family of relations living among each other, making it easier to settle disputes when they arose in the future and for keeping alliances.

During the early period of the settlement of the French, the most influential *Anishnaabe* (Algonquin) chief would be *Tessouat* The One Eyed (Clément p. 54). His people would name themselves after the great river they lived on and be called the *Kichisippirini* Great River People. For many years this one eyed chief would influence the decisions of his people. It was through the influence of *Innu* leader *Anadabijou* that *Tessouat* would join the Algonquin coalition against the *Rotinonshonni*.

However, during these trying times the greatest *Anishnaabe* (Algonquin) warrior would be *Piskeret*. Given the Christian name Simon *Piskeret,* he would be revered by all the Algonquian peoples and feared by the *Rotinonshonni*. It was said that he had once hidden himself in a woodpile in a *Kenienke:haka* village. Each time someone came out of the longhouse to look around he hit him over the head and killed him. No one in the village could ever find out where *Piskeret* was hiding. *Piskeret* would later be killed during a truce with the *Kenienke:haka* (Grassman pp. 119–120). Some say his death was an unjust one, due to a revenge killing. His death would portend to an even greater disaster that would befall the *Anishnaabe* (Algonquin) of the *Kichisippi*.

In the year 1649, the *Rotinonshonni* amalgamated their forces with the *Kenienke:haka* and *Sonotowa:haka* at the head. They attacked the *Anishnaabe* (Algonquin) along the *Kichisippi* with all of their force and might. This attack resulted in forcing many *Anishnaabe* (Algonquins) into the interior and opened up the *Kichisippi* for the *Rotinonshonni* to not only attack the French settlements around Ville Marie, but also resulted in an even greater attack against the *Wendat*. They would move in from two locations, up the *Kichisippi* and by way of the *Kaniatarowanenneh*.

The *Mi'kmaq*

The *Mi'kmaq* resided in seven districts along the North East Coast of North America. They called their territtory *Kespe'kewag* The Last Land, *Wunama'kik* Land Of Fog, *Piktuk'kik* Where There Is Noise Like Explosions, *Eskikewa'kik* Skin Dressings Territory, *Sipikne'katik* Wild Potato Area, *Kespukwitk* Land Ends and *Epexiwitk* Lying In Water (Paul p. 5). These names are very difficult to pronounce but they are all in the areas of Prince Edward Island, Cape Breton Island, Nova Scotia, New Brunswick and the upper St. Lawrence region of Quebec. Their territory was vast and plentiful. Like other Indigenous peoples, the *Mi'kmaq* would live near the ocean and mouths of rivers in the summer and move to the interior during the winter. This was to protect them from the cold winds. The *Mi'kmaq* also called themselves *Elnu* People.

The *Mi'kmaq* speak an Algonquian language similar to the *Anishnaabe* language, but different enough so they didn't completely understand each other. It is similar to the difference between French and Spanish, both Latin languages but not discernable to one another.

The *Mi'kmaq* told stories about their history and culture by way of oral tradition. This means they didn't write them down. Instead they memorized the stories and passed them down from generation to generation. The oldest stories are called *atookwakuns* in *Mi'kmaq*. It would be the elders in the villages who would tell the children how everything came to be in the world. Most often, these stories were told in the winter when it was harder to go outside. It was a way for children to be entertained as well as be educated in their traditions.

One story the *Mi'kmaq* told is how they first arrived on *Abegweit* Cradled On A Board (Prince Edward Island) by floating on a boat of ice. Perhaps they had drifted on an iceberg. No one is certain (Whitehead p. 6).

The stories that the *Mi'kmaq* liked to tell the most were about their cultural hero whom they call *Glooscap*. *Glooscap* was said to be both human and a spirit. He lived on the earth, long before the *Mi'kmaq* came into existence. It as said that one day, *Glooscap* arrived with his brother *Malsum* in *Uktamkoo* Newfoundland. It was there that *Glooscap* created the little people who looked after nature. The little people are similar to fairies and are hairy in appearance and are known to live among rocks. Today, it is believed that only children can see them. However, there is still a place in Newfoundland where non-Indigenous islanders refuse to walk because they say the little people are angry.

Glooscap then created the Marten and from that time on Marten became *Glooscap's* companion. *Glooscap* also created the *Elnu*. One day, the *Elnu* decided to leave *Uktamkoo*. They spread out across the Maritimes becoming the *Mi'kmaq*, *Malicete*, *Penobscot*, and *Passamaquoddie* peoples. *Glooscap* taught them everything they needed to know about how to survive. These Indigenous peoples are very similar to one another in their customs and language (Hill pp. 17–25).

Like other Indigenous societies, the *Mi'kmaq* had a belief that there are other worlds that exist besides the earth world. A comparison one could make of what the different worlds would represent is if one were to plant a tree with the roots of the tree going into the earth; the trunk springing up from the earth; the branches reaching the sky; and then the stars, moon and sun above. If one were to look up at the sky, this is where the characters found in many of *atookwakuns* Ancient Stories reside. The tree is an example the *Mi'kmaq* and other Aboriginal peoples use to describe how the different worlds are connected to each other. Let me explain more about these different worlds that the *Mi'kmaq* referred to as lodges.

1) The Earth Lodge is the center of all the other worlds. This is the world we human beings inhabit. It also includes the air, water, grasses, trees, and animals and is circular in its form.
2) Below the Earth Lodge lies the Root Lodge. This can be a dangerous and mysterious place for those whose spirits are able to journey out of the body. It is also where the birthing of the things within earth takes place. They then spring up into the earth lodge. Examples given are plants that grow and give us food and medicine.
3) There is also a Deep Earth Lodge where special caves exist. Within this Deep Earth Lodge the *Mi'kmaq* receive instructions while they are dreaming on how to prepare medicines. The protector of the animals also lives in this place. Whenever the *Mi'kmaq* would hunt they first sent prayers to the protector of the

animals. In return, the protector would help the humans find the animals so they could find sustenance. Whenever human beings hurt animals without reason, the protector of the animals would become angry and send sickness in return.

4) Above the Earth Lodge is the Sky Lodge. This is a place where birds like the eagle wander. The clouds, stars, sun, moon, thunders and the four winds also exist in this place.

5) The *Muntu* Spirits in this final lodge are very powerful in that they can control the weather. This is the Ancestor Lodge, a place where the spirits of those who pass from the earth end up if they are good. They travel along a trail that can be seen in the night. We call it the Milky Way. The imprint of the ancient ones from the *atookwakuns* is left in the different constellations. If some one has not being good in life the *Mi'kmaq* believe they are sent back to be born again and to learn more lessons in life (Henderson pp. 20–21).

Traditionally, the *Mi'kmaq* lived off of the plants and animals found in the forest. This included bear, moose, porcupine, hare, grouse and passenger pigeons. The passenger pigeon no longer exists, but in the past it was a main staple of food for many Indigenous societies. They were once so plentiful, that the sky would turn black when they flew over. They became extinct after the arrival of Europeans who brought guns. The English learned from the *Mi'kmaq* that if you blinded a pigeon and tied it to a stool, it would call other pigeons over. This is where we get the term 'stool pigeon' from.

There were also many plants that the *Mi'kmaq* lived off of. They included the cranberry, blueberry, strawberry and raspberry plants. The *Mi'kmaq* also fished as a means of survival. Some of the fish caught in lakes and rivers like the giant sturgeon weighed 800 lbs. Along the outlets of rivers and streams that led into the Atlantic Ocean, the *Mi'kmaq* were able to catch shellfish, lobster, crabs, salmon and eels. The *Mi'kmaq* would sail into the Atlantic Ocean in large boats made of moose skin where they could spear walrus, seals and whales. However, the most important staple of the *Mi'kmaq* diet was the salmon, which ran along rivers like the *Listiguj* that ran into the Atlantic Ocean (Leavitt pp. 9–10).

The *Mi'kmaq* lived in shelters they called *wigoums*. These were conical in shape and were made of a variety of sizes. There was an entrance and a place for a fire in the middle. The frame of the wigwam was built on spruce poles. The sides were made of birch bark sheets tied together in order to keep out the cold. They were also easy to build, take apart, and move. Some *wigoums* (wigwams) were built to hold as many as thirty people (Leavitt p. 21).

The *Mi'kmaq* constructed their main mode of transportation, the canoe, out of birch bark. These birch bark canoes were around ten to thirty feet in length. They were made higher on the sides so that water wouldn't flood them if went on the ocean (Leavitt p. 24). The *Mi'kmaq* also made boats out of moose skin. These could be made by lashing about twenty-five moose skins together. A moose skin boat could carry several families across large expanses of water. It explains how they were able to travel back and forth from *Uktamkoo* (Newfoundland) (Whitehead p. 20). The *Mi'kmaq* also made snowshoes for travel in the winter.

Mi'kmaq beliefs were similar to other Algonquin societies in that they used the sweat lodge. Their spiritual leaders were called *puoin*. It is from the root word *puoin* that we get the word powwow from. The word *puoin* is related to things that have spiritual properties within them. These *puoin* could heal the sick by using certain plants and herbs grown in the environment. Through fasting they acquired guardian spirits to help them in their healing. *Mi'kmaq* believed that everything that had life also had a spirit. This included plants, animals and human beings. Because of their beliefs, the *Mi'kmaq* treated all forms of life with respect. The power that a *Mi'kmaq* attained through fasting is called *Keskmsit*. It could come from many different living things as well as from the spirit world (Leavitt p. 10).

The encounters between *Mi'kmaq* and Europeans would change their way of life forever. There is a story the *Mi'kmaq* tell about a girl who had a dream long ago. In her dream she sees an island floating towards her. On the island there are bears climbing up and down three trees. It was not much longer after having her dream that it appeared that an island with climbing bears was seen far in the distance. As the island got close, the *Mi'kmaq* realized they were seeing a large boat with men climbing up and down ropes. These many were burly and their faces were covered with hair (Whitehead p. 8).

The *Mi'kmaq* believe that before the arrival of the European, the *Mi'kmaq* population was much larger than today. After the arrival of Europeans they began to catch strange sicknesses from these newcomers. These were measles, colds, flues, and worst of all smallpox. This resulted in the deaths of many. One *Mi'kmaq Sagamore* Chief long ago said at one time there were so many *Mi'kmaq* and other Indigenous peoples residing along the Atlantic Coast during the summer, that the fires could be seen burning at night for miles all along the beaches (Richardson pp. 43–44).

It was around the year 1612, that the great *Mi'kmaq Sagamore*, *Membertoo*, became the first *Mi'kmaq* convert to Roman Catholicism (Whitehead p. 40). This began the transition from the *Mi'kmaq* traditional belief system to Roman Catholicism. This has resulted in a long relationship between the *Mi'kmaq* and the Catholic Church that continues to this day. It also resulted in strong alliances with the Catholic French over the Protestant English during the period of warfare between the two European powers. In spite of the changes that have occurred, the *Mi'kmaq* retained their special relationship to their lands and in recent years there has been a resurgence of their traditional beliefs.

The *Mi'kmaq* relationship with the French was always good, that is until recent years. Rights promised the *Mi'kmaq* by the Federal Government over fishing, hunting and logging have led to disagreements with the descendents of French and English settlers. Originally, the French settled in the place they called Acadie. This was in what is now called *Shubenacadie* Place Where There Are Groundnuts (Nova Scotia) and *Oromucto* (New Brunswick) a *Malicete* word meaning Good River. This is in reference to the St. Johns River where both *Mi'kmaq* and *Malicete* live. It was with the English, who arrived after the French, that the *Mi'kmaq* would face the most difficulties. The arrival of the English would result in the eventual expulsion of some of the allies of the *Mi'kmaq*, the French Acadians and the near-extermination of the *Mi'kmaq* people, especially those around *Musquodobit* Rolling Out In Foam near the Atlantic Ocean.

The first treaties that the *Mi'kmaq* made with Europeans were with the French. So close were the French to the *Mi'kmaq* that they retained the *Mi'kmaq* place name *Ki peq* Where The River Narrows (Quebec). A treaty is an agreement between two peoples where both sides get something they need. Due to their relationship with the French, whenever a war took place between the French and English, the *Mi'kmaq* sided with the French. This angered the English and the *Mi'kmaq* became rivals. In retaliation the English invited the *Mi'kmaq* from *Musquodobit* to a feast and then offered their guests poisoned food, killing some of them. They also paid a bounty as a reward for killing *Mi'kmaq* in the area.

By the year 1725, the *Mi'kmaq* and the English made a truce by agreeing to a treaty. The treaty called for the *Mi'kmaq* to stop fighting the English. In return the English would not bother them when they went hunting (Paul p. 76–77). This is called a Peace and Friendship Treaty as there is no land involved in the negotiation. Today, the *Mi'kmaq* claim that they never gave up title to their lands.

Due to the continuing wars between the French and English, the treaty did not last very long. Soon after, the *Mi'kmaq* and the English began fighting each other once again. When there was peace between these two European nations there was peace for the *Mi'kmaq*. During the next war, the English General Cornwallis placed an even higher bounty for killing *Mi'kmaq,* with bounty amounts less for every child and woman killed, and higher for men. The English had a problem with retrieving the bounties; when given the chance the *Mi'kmaq* always carried off their dead with them.

In 1752, another Peace and Friendship treaty was made between the *Mi'kmaq* and English. The *Mi'kmaq Sagamore* Chief who signed the treaty was given the Christian name John Baptist Cope. The treaty promised that the *Mi'kmaq* would be able to hunt and fish in return for keeping the peace, and also trade their goods at special truck houses built for them (Paul p. 115–119). A truck house was a little trading post the English set up so that the *Mi'kmaq* could trade their furs and fish.

This treaty became important once again when the *Mi'kmaq* wanted to have their rights to the Peace and Friendship treaties affirmed by the Canadian government. A famous Supreme Court case called the Marshall Case in the 1990's, affirmed their right to fish and sell it on the market. It was heard by the Supreme Courts of Canada and based on the Peace and Friendship treaties of the past.

After the Royal Proclamation of 1763 was signed by King George III of England, the *Mi'kmaq* right to hunt and fish was supposed to be protected forever. A proclamation is legislation set down by a king that everyone is supposed to abide by. However, many of the English settlers ignored the Royal Proclamation and simply moved onto *Mi'kmaq* lands and hunted the game out.

By the year 1780, the English had allowed settlers from the United States called United Empire Loyalists to claim *Mi'kmaq* lands in Nova Scotia, Cape Breton and Prince Edward Island. They cleared the land of its forests and animals resulting in starvation for the *Mi'kmaq* (p. 185). Pretty soon, *Mi'kmaq* were begging for food from the Loyalists settlers. With their allies the French defeated years before, the *Mi'kmaq* were at the mercy of the British Crown. Like their *Anishnaabe* Brethren in Southern Ontario, the *Mi'kmaq* became subjects or wards of the Crown. They would need to ask permission to hunt and fish and because they had no written treaties for land, and they would be considered squatters on lands they had inhabited for thousands of years. Yet, through all of these hardships the *Mi'kmaq* continued to survive as a people.

The *Wendat* Islanders or Huron

By 1611 the *Wendat* Islanders (Huron) had become the main players in the fur trade after fifty of their leaders visited Samuel De Champlain at Ville Marie (Montreal) They had arrived to ask him to by-pass the *Anishnaabe* (Algonquin) and make the *Wendat* the main people to trade with. Who were these people who named themselves after a Great Turtle whom they believed supported the earth like an island between waters?

The *Wendat* migrated with other Iroquoian peoples thousands of years ago from the *Mississippi* (Long River) Valley to their territory called *Taronto* Place of the Fish Weirs, situated between Lake Huron, the Trent water basin and Lake Ontario. In fact the languages of the *Wendat* and *Kenienke:haka* Flint People (Mohawk) are quite similar. There are some *Wendat* oral traditions that mention that some of them were living along the *Kaniatarowanenneh* River St. Lawrence R. and along the northern banks of *Kanontario* Beautiful Lake Ontario and then fled the *Rotinonshonni* Longhouse People (Iroquois) whom lived south of them.

Kenienke:haka tradition also claims that during a dream feast an *onkwe honwe* Real Person of the *Wendat* nation dreamt he had to kill a *Kenienké* Flint (Mohawk) Man. While playing out the role that was to be interpreted by another, he got carried away with his task and instead of acting the situation out as was custom, killed the *Kenienké* man. This led to conflict between the once closely related peoples. Another tradition has *Wendat* moving west from *Hochelega* Place Of The Council Fire (Montreal) after being attacked by the *Anishnaabe* First Human (Algonquin peoples). They finally made a truce with the *Anishnaabe* and settled in a peaceful alliance with them in their territory north of *Kanontario*. Regardless of which story is the truer one, for they may all be true, the *Wendat* have inhabited the northern region of *Kanontario* Lake Ontario for many years in the place they called *Taranto* Place Of The Fish Weirs.

The *Wendat* have an oral tradition that preceded their settling in *Taranto*. Long ago, there were two worlds that existed, one in the sky and the earth. The world above in the sky held all of the essences of the living beings that would that would come to life on the earth world. These essences were known as *oia:ron* or *oki* Spirit, and had human-like qualities.

The world that the *Wendat* would one day inhabit would be on Great Turtle's Back, now North America. Before the Great Turtle gave his body for the *Wendat* to live on there was only water. The only beings able to survive were those that could live in or on the water or could fly. One day, a young female being in the Sky World, decided to cut some corn stocks instead of simply plucking them from the sole patch that existed. Once the corn stocks were cut down they could never grow again. Some of her brothers became angry and so they threw the young woman through a hole in the sky world into the abyss. In her hands were the corn stocks she had cut down, along with the beans, squash and tobacco she was able to pull from the ground before falling. These items would become very important for the survival of the *Wendat* later on. The *Wendat* refer to the woman who fell from the sky by the name *Aataentsic* Ancient Female. Far below *Aataentsic* was only water.

As the young woman fell through the sky, some of the waterfowl who were able to survive on the water suddenly looked up. There were ducks, herons, and loons. They could see her falling towards them so they flew up and surrounded her. They created a cushion for her to land on; however, their wings were getting tired of holding her in the air. Great Turtle arrived and told them to put her on his back. He said he would relieve them and hold her. Then toad arrived and said he would dive down into the water and get some earth from the bottom. When he came up, he had a mouthful of dirt and then spit it out on the turtles back. He told the young woman to sprinkle the dirt everywhere she walked.

As the young woman walked round the turtle's back, she planted the corn, beans, squash and tobacco everywhere she went. However, the woman was still very lonely. One day she discovered twin boys. These boys grew very quickly. One of the brothers created all of the living things on earth including the *Wendat*. The other brother tried to do the same thing and instead created monkeys instead of humans. And so each brother made different things, some that were good and some that were bad. The first brother made everything that the *Wendat* could use to survive while the other made things that could harm them (Barbeau p. 10).

The *Wendat* creation story is similar to the creation story of other Iroquoian peoples with some minor differences. It explains that within the *Wendat* world view some plants and animals are very important to them and provide the means for their survival. Certain plants and animals provide food and as in the story sacrifice themselves on behalf of the *Wendat*. In exchange the *Wendat* must give thanks.

After the good brother had created the *Wendat* and they moved to *Taranto*, they split up but remained confederated into four or possibly five groups. These were based on a clan system. It included the *Atinniawenton* They Are From The Bear Country; *Atingeenonniahak* They Used To Make Cord; *Arendaeronnon* People At The Rock; *Atahontaerat* Two White Ears Of Corn; and the *Ataroncharonon* People In The Swamp (Steckley pp. 2–3). Being in a clan is like having a membership in an extended family. Everyone in the family belongs to the same clan. In the *Wendat* culture the clan went through the mother's side of the family; therefore, they are called a matrilineal society. It means that once born they belong to their mother's clan; for instance if a *Wendat* mother was Rock Clan, her children were members of that clan. A *Wendat* person could never marry someone who was a member of the same clan. There are some oral traditions that say that the *Rotinonshonni* Longhouse People (Iroquois Confederacy) was modeled after the *Wendat* Confederacy. That was because according to some *Rotinonshonni* oral traditions a Peacemaker who was born *Wendat,* was able to confederate the *Wendat* people after they became separated and then traveled south confederating the *Rotinonshonni* and even other nations such as the Neutral near *Onagara* (Niagara Falls).

The *Wendat* place of residence was the *Ganonchia* Longhouse. This structure was made of cedar slabs tied together on an arching wooden frame. The Longhouses could be over 100 feet long and could hold as many as ten families or more. These families lived across a fire from one another. On each side of the fire, there were raised platforms, which they would sleep on. Bearskins were used as blankets, especially in the cold winters. There was also a storage room at one end of the Longhouse where preserved corn could be hung and dried (Trigger pp. 59–60). During one period in history when they were at war, the *Wendat* built palisades around their villages of Longhouses to protect them. This probably occurred during their wars with the *Anishnaabe* and *Rotinonshonni*.

The *Wendat* spoke an Iroquoian language. This means there were other Indigenous peoples who spoke a similar language such the five nations of the *Rotinonshonni* Longhouse People; the *Attiwandaronk* Neutrals; the *Etionnontateronon* Tobacco Nation and others.

There is a stereotype about Indigenous peoples in North America, which is that they were solely hunters and gatherers. This was true for a minority of Indigenous peoples who lived in the far North and could not plant due to the short summer season. However, most Indigenous peoples like the *Wendat* were involved in agriculture. In fact seventy percent of foods grown and produced helping to feed the world originally came from the Indigenous peoples of the Americas. Some examples are potatoes, tomatoes, chocolate, chewing gum, corn flakes, cranberry, amaranth, cassava, and many more. The *Wendat* were no exception and have sometimes been referred to as farmers of the north (Trigger p. 26). Their main staples were corn, beans, squash, and tobacco. They were influential in showing Algonquin peoples like the *Odawa* how to farm. In fact in some villages the *Odawa* set up their own Longhouses beside *Wendat* Longhouses. The *Odawa* Traders were the main middle-men in trade between the *Wendat* and other *Anishnaabe* besides themselves.

The *Wendat* followed a yearly cycle of ceremonies based on a moon calendar that changed with each lunar cycle. A harvest moon for instance might be in October. There would be a great feast held at that time which was a form of thanksgiving. During harvest all of the food would be collected and either eaten or stored in storage pits to preserve it throughout the winter when food became scarce. After harvest, deer meat would become the most important food source. By the time spring arrived, *Wendat* would begin tapping maple trees to provide maple syrup. Then berry picking and fishing would take place.

All of these activities centered on the disappearance and return of a new moon every 26 days or so. The stars were also important in helping to teach the *Wendat* what their duties were each season. Much like the moon, star constellations move through the sky appearing and disappearing in cycles. When a new star constellation would appear the *Wendat* would have a story to tell about it and then prepare for a new function.

Each Mid-Winter (February), the *Wendat* participated in dream interpretation. They believed that dreams were very important to understand. Dreams could foretell the future and even cause illness if not dealt with properly. The *Wendat* believed that sometimes people held things inside of them. These suppressed thoughts and feelings would sometimes be expressed in dreams. They would then play a game similar to charades and have someone act out their dreams. This would help them interpret what the dream really meant. By acting out the dream, the *Wendat* believed that they would remain healthy in mind, body and spirit. (Trigger p. 114) Some of the ideas in modern psychology are similar to *Wendat* dream interpretation therapy.

When the French explorer Jacques Cartier sailed up the *Kaniatarowanenneh* River Of The Longhouse People (Iroquois) during his first two voyages in 1534 and 1535, he encountered various peoples who spoke a similar language. They could have been *Wendat, Kenienke:haka* or a separate but similar group of people. There is a good chance that some of them were *Wendat* and probably of the *Atingeenoniak* Cord Clan. This may have been because the *Atingeenoniak* arrived north of *Kanontario* Beautiful Lake and west of the *Kaniatarow-anenneh* some time between the arrival of Cartier and another French explorer named Samuel De Champlain, who arrived seventy years later (Trigger p. 157).

After the arrival of the French, the *Atingeenoniak* became their main trading partners. What we do know is that by the time Samuel De Champlain arrival around 1603 the *Wendat* were well settled in the territory of *Taranto*. However, they maintained a strong connection to the area along the *Kaniatarowanenneh* where the French would settle. There is a good chance that several groups once inhabited the area with the *Atingeenoniak* being one.

It was not long after Champlain's arrival that the French saw an opportunity to do business with the *Wendat*. Champlain offered to help them in their wars with the *Rotinonshonni* in return for their assistance in trade. It is during thus time that some *Wendat, Anishnaabe* (Algonquin) and French traveled towards a lake now named after Champlain, and attacked a party of *Kenienke:haka* one of the five nations that made up the *Rotinonshonni*. Champlain had a strange powerful new weapon called the arquebus. Not long after the attack the *Rotinonshonni* were acquiring their own arquebuses from the Dutch who had arrived by traveling up the *Mahacanituk* Wolf River: a river that would later be named after Henry Hudson. This attack would have dire consequences for the livelihood of the *Wendat, Anishnaabe* (Algonquin) and even the French. However, the greatest threat to the *Wendat* would not be the *Rotinonshonni*, nor would it be the arquebus, but rather disease brought to them by the Catholic priests. An estimated 20,000 *Wendat* would die this way leaving about 10,000 to fend off future attacks from the *Rotinonshonni* (Trigger p. 233).

With the *Rotinonshonni* Longhouse People (Iroquois) acquiring the arquebus from the Dutch, the *Wendat* needed the French to trade with in order to acquire some of their own. A condition the French made in order for the *Wendat* to receive the arquebus was that they first had to convert to Roman Catholicism. This meant in order to have an equal chance against the *Rotinonshonni* they would have to forfeit their own beliefs in exchange for the beliefs of the French. The result was that some were willing to do so, at first just a few.

Unfortunately this resulted in two things happening which would have a profound affect on the *Wendat*. The first being it created two classes of *Wendat*: those who remained traditional and egalitarian, and a more wealthy class of Roman Catholic *Wendat* who benefited from the trade. And second, it divided the *Wendat* amongst themselves. The bickering and divisions that would result made the *Wendat* ineffective against an attack by their enemy the *Rotinonshonni*. The Priests had informed the *Wendat* that their God of war led by Jesus was punishing them for not accepting the Roman Catholic religion and if they accepted Him, God would help them beat their enemies and cure them of their illness. This is reflected in Jesuit father Piersons explanation of Jesus 'as the one who bears the war bundle':

I am talking now of one who bears the reed mat of war, Jesus. He returned to the sky. He goes about overcoming them, killing the spirit and with it bringing the death of all sinning. All of us are enemies of the spirit. Jesus, the master will help us. He will wish that we overcome the spirit too. We will have the forces and ability by means of attachment to him. Jesus will also do this. Onontio (the French Governor) will overcome the Seneca when he goes with his troops. The one who bears the reed mat of war will do it, as I have said this day. All overcoming is such. We should congratulate Jesus, our master, as he overcame them. It would encourage our forces, so it would be certain that we will overcome the spirit who bears us ill will, and sinning. He fights for us also that he discourages those spirits who are our enemies, who pursue us and bring us bad fortune. On this day he will take the group to the sky. He goes about seizing them, making them disappear, when he overcomes them (Steckley pp. 478–509).

In spite of this most *Wendat* remained true to their beliefs until the final attacks by the *Rotinonshonni*. Previous to the attacks, only about 500 converted to Roman Catholicism. After the attacks the *Wendat* that remained traditional were adopted among the five *Rotinonshonni* nations while the mostly Catholic *Wendat* sought refuge with the priests. Unfortunately for the *Wendat* who remained behind, the priests, although remaining well supplied by the French, didn't have enough supplies to provide for the *Wendat* so they starved.

Many of the surviving *Wendat* had first fled to Christian Island, and then moved once again to live with their allies the *Odawa* on Manitoulin Island. The priests promised that if they followed them they would find safety and refuge.

The remaining Catholic *Wendat* settled at a place they would call *Wendake* above *Ke piq* The River Narrows (Quebec) on the *Kaniatarowanenneh* River Of The Longhouse People (St. Lawrence River). Most of these remained Roman Catholic. Those *Wendat* who were not adopted by the *Rotinonshonni* moved to the southern end of *Michigami* Great Lake (Lake Michigan). They became known as *Wyandot* Floating Islanders instead of *Wendat* Islanders. This meant they were now wanderers without a homeland on the Great Turtle's back. In later years, many of them would be forced by the government of the United States to move to Kansas and Oklahoma, while others still remain in *Wendake* or around *Michigami*.

Learning Activity

1. Look at a map and place where the *Mi'kmaq*, *Anishnaabe* and *Wendat* were situated.

2. What were the motivations for the Aboriginal peoples in the text in trading with the French? What were the motivations of the French to trade with the Indigenous Peoples?

3. What were the main cultural differences between the Algonquin Peoples and the Iroquoian Peoples?

4. From your understanding of relations between Newcomers and Indigenous Peoples, are there any differences from what you learned in the past and what you have read here?

Review

1. Name the different peoples in the text? Provide the Indigenous names, their meanings, and the names they have been given by Europeans?

2. Name the different places in the text. Provide the Aboriginal names, their meanings, and the names given by Europeans?

3. Who were some of the key figures in history mentioned in the text?

4. Compare this chapter with chapter four. What are the different perspectives given of events in the same time period by the *Anishnaabe*, *Wendat* and *Rotinonshonni*?

References

Barbeau, Marius. (1960). Huron-Wyandot Traditional Narratives. Ottawa: National Museum of Canada.

Benton-Benai, Eddie (1988). The Mishomis Book: *the voice of the Ojibwa*. St. Paul, Minnesota:Red School House.

Clément, Daniel. (1996). The Algonquins.

Mercury Series Canadian Ethnology Service Paper 130. Ottawa: Canadian Museum of Civilization.

Grassman, Tom. (1969). The Mohawk Indians And Their Valley: *being a chronology documentary record to the end of 1963.* Schenectady, NY: Hugo Photography and Printing Co.

Henderson, James Sa'ke'j (1992). Algonquin Spirituality: *balancing the opposites.* Mi'kmaq Studies: University College of Cape Breton.

Hill, Kay. (1970). Glooscap and his Magic. Toronto, Montreal: McClelland and Stewart. Leavitt, R. M. (1985). The Micmac. Nova Scotia: Fitzhenry & Whiteside Limited.

Paul, Daniel. (1993). We Were Not The Savages.

Halifax, Nova Scotia: Nimbus Publishing.

Richardson, Boyce. (1993). People of Terra Nullius. Vancouver/Toronto: Douglas & McIntyre.

Steckley, John. (1992). The warrior and the lineage: Jesuit use of Iroquoian images to communicate Christianity. *Ethnohistory,* 3(4). Duke University Press.

Thomas, Jake. (1992). personal correspondence. Oshwegan: The Iroquois Institute.

Trigger, B.G. (1969). The Huron: Farmers of the North. New York: Holt, Rinehart and Winston.

Whitehead, Ruth. (1991). The Old Man Told Us: *excerpts from Micmac history 1500–1950.* Halifax: Nimbus Publishing.

Steckley, John. Wendat Dialects and the Development of the Huron Alliance. [On-line]. www.wyandot.org

Trigger, Bruce. (1987). The Children of Aataentsic. Montreal: McGill-Queen's University Press.

Trigger, Bruce. (1989). Natives and Newcomers: *Canada's heroic age revisited.* Montreal & Kingston: McGill-Queen's University Press.

ENCOUNTERS BETWEEN INDIGENOUS PEOPLES AND NEWCOMERS IN EASTERN CANADA: A KENIENKÉHAKA PERSPECTIVE

Introduction

As we continue to look at first encounters between newcomers and Indigenous peoples, we will explore Canadian history written from an Indigenous perspective by utilizing both the oral and written traditions of the *Kenienké:haka* Flint People (Mohawk). All Iroquoian peoples name themselves from a derivation of the words *onkwe:honwe* Real People where we will begin the story as there is uncertainty in the early encounters between Iroquoian peoples and the French, which Iroquoian people held precedence around the area of Montreal. Most of the early pre-encounter stories come from the *Kenienké:haka*. This will include some conflicts between the *onkwe:honwe* and *anishnaabe*, and how events that occurred were affected with the arrival of the French, English, and Dutch. First I will start with a brief history of the *Otsiré;haka* and then the *Rotinonshonni* Longhouse Peoples (Iroquois Confederacy) pre and post contact, to which the *Kenienké:haka* Flint Peoples (Mohawk) belong. Primarily, this section will be about the first encounter between the French explorer Samuel De Champlain and the *Kenienké:haka* in 1609 shaping the future of both peoples. The preliminary will include information on the *Kenienké:haka* Flint Peoples (Mohawk); the *Rotinonshonni* Longhouse Peoples (Five Nation Iroquois); the *Mississauaga* Big Lake Outlet Peoples (Ojibwa); the *Shawanee* (Southerners); and events that have shaped the destinies of these Indigenous nations. The section called *Sawiskera Gains Control* comes from my book *The Rotinonshonni: A Traditional Iroquoian History Through the Eyes of Teharonhia:wako and Sawiskera*.

Preliminary

Many years before the arrival of newcomers from Europe, there was a period of conflict that prevailed in north-east North America. Central to these conflicts were the *Kenienké:haka* or Flint People (Mohawk); *Oneota:haka* Standing Stone Peoples (Oneida); *Onondaka:haka* Peoples of the Hills (Onondaga); *Kaokwa:haka* Mucky Lake Peoples (Cayuga); and *Sonontowa:haka* Peoples of the Great Hill (Seneca). According to their oral traditions, these Five Nations later to be known as the Iroquois, would unite and name themselves *Rotinonshonni* Long House People. It would be a *Wendat* People of the Island (Huron) person, named *Tekanawita* Between Two Streams, along with a *Kenienké:ha* Flint Person named *Ayenwatha* He Was Awoke and a woman from the *Kakwaka* Neutral Nation named *Jakonsasé* Face Like a Cat, that would bind the Five Nations into a confederacy living in peace among themselves and their neighbours that lasted for five hundred years. This peace was called *Kaianeré:kowa* The Great Law of Peace.

The *Rotinonshonni* symbolically planted a Great White Pine Tree of Peace at *Kanata:kowa* Big Village, in the territory of the *Onondaka:haka* People of the Hills. At that place they buried their weapons of war. They explained the meaning of the union of the Five Nations by use of metaphors, such as sharing from the same kettle and eating the beaver tail without drawing blood. This meant everyone could hunt in the same territory without fear of being killed. *Jakonsasé* helped the women from the different clan families decide which chosen representative *royaner* They of the Good Mind (traditional chief) would sit in council at *Kanata:kowa* village. The head woman of each of the clans chose fifty men from the Five Nations. Once chosen these men were to meet whenever necessary at *Kanata:kowa* village, to decide the affairs of *Rotinonshonni,* relaying the voices of the men's and women's council of each nation in their meeting. The women would have the power to remove any *royaner* leader who didn't do the will of the people. Many years later a sixth Nation called *Scaroon* Hemp Shirt Peoples (Tuscarora) would join the five, who then became known as the Six Nations confederacy.

Something we should understand is that some of the names of the Nations in use today are not the ones the Indigenous peoples knew themselves by. Many of the names given came from misunderstandings in translation by Dutch, French, or English colonizers. Two examples are the names Mohawk for the *Kenienké:haka* and Seneca for the *Sonontowa:haka.*

Years ago, when the Dutch first traveled up the *Mahicantuk Sipi* Wolf River (Hudson River) they encountered a group of peoples who were known as *Mahican* Wolf Peoples. The *Mahican* spoke a different language from the *Rotinonshonni.* They asked the *Mahican* for the name of the peoples that lived next to them. The *Mahican* said that they were the *Mohawkwa* Bear People. In later years, after 1666, the English displaced the Dutch and they shortened the name to Mohawk. The Dutch had also asked the *Mahican* about the peoples who live next to the *Mohawkwa.* They replied with *Assiniga* Standing Stone Peoples in their language. It is in actual fact the name for the *Oneota:haka.* As the English learned the names of the different nations that made up the *Rotinonshonni* living west of the *Kenienké:haka* (Mohawk), the *Sonontowa:haka,* who were furthest west were renamed Seneca from the name *Assinika* Standing Stone in the *Mahican* language. Today when members of the *Rotinonshonni* utilize the names given to them such as Mohawk and Seneca, they do so only when they speak English, but not when they speak their own languages. Therefore, the *Sonontowa:haka* also refer to themselves as Seneca, just as the *Kenienké:haka* refer to themselves as Mohawk as these were the names given to them by the Dutch and English.

It would be after the arrival of the French who sailed up the *Kaniatariowanenneh* River Of The *Rotinonshonni* (St. Lawrence River) in 1534 and the Dutch who sailed up the *Mahicantuk* Wolf River (Hudson River) in 1609, that great changes occurred to the *Rotinonshonni* and other Indigenous peoples in the area. All would suffer through periods of warfare like they had never seen before. Disease spread rapidly among them resulting in the disappearance of many of the Indigenous Nations. Either warfare or disease would displace the cousins of the *Rotinonshonni* that lived along the *Kaniatariowanenneh,* with some joining their brethren south and others moving west.

The French had referred to these peoples as Canadians, from the Iroquoian word *Kanata* meaning village. Later, it would be the French who would take up the designation Canadién. Finally, Canadian would be the designation for all peoples living in Canada.

After becoming involved in wars between the French and English and then the British and Americans, the *Rotinonshonni* would become divided, and the kettle that they had all once eaten from would be shattered. This meant that they no longer shared with one another under the *Kaianeré:kowa* Great Law of Peace. Soon after, the *Kenienké:haka* would suffer from the dispossession of their country which they once called *Tonanachi* Between Two Mountains (Mohawk Valley). Most would be forced to live in British North America and later the new country called Canada. Other members of the *Rotinonshonni* would either move to the other side of *Kanontario* Beautiful Lake or remain in the United States.

The *Anishnaabe* First Humans, once rivals of the *Rotinonshonni* and involved in the dispossession of their cousins from the *Kaniatarioweneh* River, would also suffer from the same fate. Some of them would remain behind and be referred to as Algonquin by the French explorer Samuel De Champlain, while others would move up the *Kichisippi* Great River (Ottawa River) and settle there or continue to travel west. Eventually, they were divided further to become the *Odawa* Traders, *Ojibwa* Roasted Words (shortened dialect) and *Pottawatomie* Fire Keepers. The latter three would one day align under a great leader named *Pontiac* and force the King of England into making a concession that is still important for Indigenous peoples in Canada. It is called the Royal Proclamation of 1763.

The Royal Proclamation of 1763, according to the King of England, George III, affirmed the rights of Indigenous peoples to their lands west of the Appalachian Mountains. Today in Canada, many Indigenous peoples still believe it acknowledges their rights to the lands they live on. The King of England based the Royal Proclamation on something called the doctrine of discovery. This means that Indigenous peoples' rights to their lands are acknowledged, but with limitations. Both the British Crown and the United States and later the Government of Canada granted themselves greater rights to the lands of Indigenous peoples than the Indigenous peoples had. According to the Royal Proclamation of 1763, the Indigenous peoples have the right to live a subsistence way of life meaning to hunt and fish, but do not have full ownership of their lands. Nonetheless, in order for the British Crown to acquire land from Indigenous peoples, they must negotiate with them first. This is called treaty making. Once treaties were signed Indigenous peoples retained a 'usufructuary right' to the land. This means the right to live off of the land but not own it. Of course the Indigenous peoples never saw it that way. They believed that after negotiating treaties, they were allowing settlers to live among them meaning that they remained the true title holders. In spite of the differences in interpretation between the two points of view, all subsequent treaties for land signed between the British Crown, the later Canadian Government and with the different Indigenous Nations, would be based on the Royal Proclamation of 1763. Therefore, it is an important document for understanding the rights and limitations that Indigenous peoples have to their lands and its meaning in law. As to whether Indigenous peoples have more than a usufructuary right is still being sorted out in Canada? The Royal Proclamation was also a catalyst for the Americans to leave British North America and fight for their independence, By British law, they were forbidden to expand west without the Crowns consent. Many of the American founding fathers were rich land holders and speculators and saw the profits to be made by taking over Indigenous peoples lands by defeating them and forcing them into making treaties and then moving the rest west. Although taxation was a pretext for leaving British North America, land was the main issue. After the War of Independence, the Royal Proclamation of 1763 was revoked by the Americans and even though treaty making resumed, it was only to legalize the defeat of the Indigenous peoples who lived on the land. Few would be allowed to remain in their homelands in the east and many would be removed first to Kansas and later Oklahoma.

What happened to the *Rotinonshonni* after joining the British and fighting the Americans during the American Revolutionary War? The thirteen colonies would win and become the United States of America, taking with them most of the *Oneota:haka* and *Scaroon with them.* The *Kenienké:haka, Onontowaaka:haka* and *Sonontowa:haka* who had fought on the side of the British, saw most of their lands given away by the British in a secret meeting in Paris, France between the British and Americans in 1782. The British, knowing they had sold out their allies to the Americans, offered to purchase land for the *Rotinonshonni* in Upper Canada (Ontario) from the *Mississauaga* Great Water Outlet Peoples *Ojibwa* First Humans in the place that is now called Ontario from the name Beautiful lake.

After the Treaty of Paris a British General named Fredrick Haldimand, asked four *Ojibwa Ogima* (leaders) if he could buy some of their land so that the *Rotinonshonni* would have a place to live on. Haldimand then told a *Kenienké:ha* Flint Person (Mohawk) war chief named Joseph Brant, who had represented the *Rotinonshonni* in council with the British, that he would give the *Rotinonshonni all* of the land six miles on each side of the *Ohioke* Beautiful River (Grand River) between Lake Erie and Lake Ontario, to replace the land they had lost in the meeting in Paris, France between Great Britain and the United States (Kelsey p. 351).

A *Kenienké* Mohawk war chief named Joseph Brant brought many members of the *Rotinonshonni* with him along with his English friends who had sided with the British during the war. These Englishmen were called United Empire Loyalists. Brant thought he could lease land to them to support his peoples. Instead the British told him that the land didn't really belong to the *Rotinonshonni* to lease as the British Crown invoked the Royal Proclamation on them limiting their rights as fee simple owners. The Loyalists soon started to push the *Rotinonshonni* off their new lands, eventually forcing them away from the town Joseph Brant had founded, named Brantford. Today, the *Rotinonshonni* live on a small reserve named Six Nations in Southern Ontario. Joseph Brant is accused by his peoples of helping to squander away much of the land once promised by Haldimand.

Things would not go much better for the *Mississauaga Ojibwa*. A British soldier killed *Wabikinine* White Eagle the *Ojibwa Ogima* Chief who had allowed Haldimand to purchase land from them on behalf of the *Rotinonshonni* after he tried to stop some of the British soldiers from molesting his daughter. His people lost their *Mississauaga* Big Water Outlet village, now *Mississauaga* Ontario, called *Missinik* Credit Village to the loyalists, and had to ask Joseph Brant's people for a place for his people to live. Today, the *Mississauaga* Big Water Outlet Peoples live next to the *Rotinonshonni* at New Credit reserve, by Six Nations reserve in Ontario (Smaltz, pp. 145–146).

By the year 1812, the British would be asking the *Rotinonshonni*, *Mississauaga* and those Indigenous peoples living close to the border between the United States and British North America, to fight for them in another war against the Americans. Once again, the British promised a homeland to those Indigenous peoples who fought with them against the Americans. Fearful of the intentions of the Americans more than they were of the British, over fifteen thousand Indigenous warriors would volunteer to fight. The greatest of them all was *Tecumseh* Panther In The Sky, a *Shawnee* (southerner) and leader from the *Ohio* Beautiful River, who fought the Americans only to have the British close the doors of a fort on him and his men while seeking refuge, during the battle of the Fallen Timbers. Tecumseh would later be killed on the Thames River, in Southern Ontario, when a British General named Proctor fled the battlefield leaving Tecumseh with four hundred of his men alone against an army of three thousand American soldiers under Henry Harrison who would one day become President of the United States.

The greatest battles for survival lay ahead for not only the *Rotinonshonni,* but also the *Mississauaga* and other Indigenous peoples in British North America and later Canada. It would not come through the barrel of gun but rather through the point of a pen and would be called the Indian Act. Below is a story based on oral traditions of the first encounters between the newcomers, the *Kenienké:haka* Flint Peoples and the other nations of the *Rotinonshonni.* The United States would refer to their policies based on doctrine of discovery as Manifest Destiny. That is, white Christian Americans were predestined to take away the lands of Indigenous non-Christians by god and the Indians were to be considered the White Man's Burden to be destroyed or civilized, Christianized and educated in the white man's ways. Here is a *Rotinonshonni* story of how these things came to be.

The Coming of the Light Skinned Beings

After a Great Peace had occurred, the *onkwe honwe* Real People of the *Rotiononhsonni* felt safe to travel anywhere without having to worry about being killed. Some of the *Kenienké:haka* had moved to the North to a great river that led into the sea they called *Kaniatariowanenneh* River of the *Rotinonshonni*. There they resided for many years, living in peace. They built villages all along the river where they hunted, fished and grew their three mothers - corn, beans and squash. The main village of the northern *Kenienké:haka* was on an island where the great river divided into two. The village was situated by a mountain on the island and was the place where the northern *Kenienké:haka* had their council fire. This was a mixed village of people from various *Rotinonshonni* nations and even possibly some *Wendat* Islanders (Wendat). Over the years they had become somewhat autonomous and they became known as the *Otsiré:haka*, the Peoples of the Council Fire (Hochelega, now Montreal).

The south river had rapids and a lake on one side which led into great bodies of water that were like oceans and a few days journey away. The first of these lakes was situated above the territory of the *Onontakaka haka*, *Kaokwa:haka* and *Sonontowa:haka* and was called *Kanontario* Beautiful Lake (Lake Ontario). At its most western part, it divided the country of the *Kakwa*s (Neutrals) where *Jakonsasé* resided, between the first great lake and the second great lake by the falls named *Onakara* (Niagara Falls). Most of the *Wendat* had moved north above *Kanontario* years before, the latter being situated in the north. Their cousins the *Tionontaté* Blue Mountain Peoples (Tobacco) lived near them. For many changes of the seasons, the *onkwe honwe* Real Peoples (All Iroquois persons) remained at peace with one another and their neighbours.

Another people who spoke a different language and had different customs lived near the great body of water to the east. These peoples were more proficient at hunting than the *onkwe honwe* and were therefore better in the use of the bow and arrow. They called themselves *Anishnaabe* First Humans. They also lived in abundance with all their needs taken care of.

Anishnaabe spiritual leaders had great spiritual powers and could communicate easily with the ancient spirits in the Sky World whom they called *Manito*. Some of these ancient spirits were good, while others were evil and could do harm. One day, their spiritual leaders began to have dreams about a terrible calamity that would occur if they remained where they were. While they were communicating with the ancient ones, as was their custom, it was said that seven spiritual beings came out of the ocean to warn them and tell them what they were to do in order to survive. They referred to these as the Seven Fires or Prophets. They had been told that they would have to leave their lands and move west if they were going to continue to survive. If they didn't, they would suffer like they had never suffered before (Benton-Benai, p. 95). Some decided to leave, while others stayed behind. Slowly they began their journey toward the west. They would have to travel through the *Otsiré:haka* country. Both the *Kenienké:haka* and the *Anishnaabe* had known of each other; however, they had remained out of each other's way after the Great Peace.

The *Kenienké:haka* had always let the *Anishnaabe* hunt in their territory, as was the custom under the Great Peace. They referred to them as *Atirontok* Bark Eaters because of the designs they made with the bark of their teeth. The *Atirontok* didn't respect the *Kenienké:haka*, because they felt that they were not true men - not good in war and hunting. The *Anishnaabe* felt that the *Kenienké-haka* women had too much power for the men to be useful. Nonetheless, the two peoples traded with one another. The *Kenienké:haka* would trade their tobacco, corn, beans and squash for the furs and meat of the *Atirontok*.

From the perspective of the *Kenienké:haka*, it was at that time that *Sawiskera* Cold As Ice (Evil Spirit) blew light skinned beings over the water to his brother *Teharonhia:wako* He Looks To The Sky (Good Spirit) Turtle Island (North America). These twins were a part of their creation story and influenced what happened on the earth.

In the *Rotinonshonni* tradition, from the time of creation these two brothers had fought against one another over control of the world. *Sawiskera* vowed to disrupt the *onkwe honwe* Real Humans (Iroquois) and the rest of the creative works of his brother *Teharonhia:wako*. *Teharonhia:wako* had created everything to perfection until his brother, Sawiskera, tried to control or destroy it. In a short time, *Sawiskera* would send a great white wind from one end of *Teharonhia:wako's* island (North America) to the other. So powerful was his wind that many of the *onkwe:honwe* would be destroyed by disease, warfare and alcohol. Many were left with doubts about who they were, and they turned against the things that *Teharonhia:wako* had taught their ancestors (Jacob Thomas, 1994, Great Law Recital).

One day, some of the cousins of the *Atirontok* named the *Mi'kmaq* saw three trees on an island, with bears climbing from ropes, sailing down the great river. When they landed, it was discovered that they were not bears or trees at all, but rather men with light skin who sailed in a great canoe that had wings which seemed to allow it to fly through the water (Whitehead p. 8).

As it sailed down the *Kaniatarowaneneh,* one of the *Kenienké:haka Royaner* Good Minded (leaders) went out to meet the light-skinned strangers just as these strangers were putting up a post that appeared to point to the four directions. This was close to *Tekiatontari:kon* Where Two Waterways Come Together (Quebec City).

The *royaner* pointed to the sign and asked the strangers, "Why are you putting up that post?"

A man named Jacques answered using sign language, "There is no harm; it is only a beacon for our ship so that others can come and trade with you."

The two men shook hands and became friends.

The *royaner* didn't know that Jacques had claimed the land for his King and spiritual leaders; the marker meant that they now believed that they possessed the land because the *onkwe;honwe* were pagans and not Christians.

The *royaner* said to Jacques, "Come to our village." *Kanata* was the term he used for the village.

Jacques thought to himself, "This country must be called Canada. When I go back I will tell my King that I have discovered Canada and that the peoples must be called Canadians."

The *royaner* introduced the strangers to his village and cured them of a terrible sickness with the boiled leaves of a cedar or spruce tree.

One day, Jacques said to the sons of the *royaner*, "would you like to see our ship?"

The two sons were thrilled to see the great sailing ship and replied, "Yes, that would be great!"

As soon as they boarded the vessel, they were captured and put in chains. Jacques and the two sons then sailed away.

The *royaner* thought he would never see his sons again. However, many moons later, the great canoe with wings returned with his sons safely inside.

Upon their return, the sons said to the *royaner*, "Father, we have been to far-off lands where a war-like people live. They are very powerful, with some having great wealth while others are starving to death."

The *royaner* thought to himself, "How could they let their own peoples starve?"

The *royaner* could have killed the strangers with the light skin. However, he knew it was wrong to kill, for he believed in the Great Peace. Instead, he fed them and looked after them through a harsh winter. One day, he believed he was safe after all he had done for the strangers.

Jacques said to him, "We will be leaving soon. We would like you to come on board our ship for a final get-together."

The *royaner* replied to Jacques, "I will miss you when you are gone."

As soon as Jacques and the *royaner* boarded the vessel, the *royaner* was captured; they sailed off.

The *Kenienké-haka* men, seeing what had happened, tried to stop the great canoe and yelled, "*Akohanna, Akohanna*." This was an old Turtle Clan title for the *royaner* who wore the antlers of the deer (Shea pp. 116–123).

That was the last that they saw of their *royaner*. However in the future, they would be warned that there were strangers who did not understand the meaning behind the Great Peace.

Not long after that time, more strangers arrived who made camp close to the Great Body of Water where the *Kaniatarowaneneh* River of the *Rotinonshonni* ended. The *Atirontok* who lived near the ocean began to die off from strange maladies for which they could find no cure. They decided to heed their spiritual leaders' warning and began to travel west in large numbers. As they traveled, they entered the territory of the northern *Kenienké-haka*. They referred to the *Kenienké-haka* as *Mundua*, or People Who were Very Spiritual (Warren pp 77–80).

They decided that they would have to destroy the *Kenienké-haka* if they were to live in this country. They concluded that they would have to attack during the night, as they knew that the *Kenienké-haka* would never prepare themselves for a night attack for they refused to fight at night.

One night, they struck at the village by the mountain, taking the *Kenienké:haka* by surprise. There, they killed many *Kenienké:haka* and captured many others.

For the first time in a long time, the *Kenienké:haka* had to fight to survive. They hid their women in pits as they defended their land. Some escaped, while others were adopted into the *Atirontok* Martin Clan and made into warriors. Those who remained were forced to pay tribute, sometimes giving their wives as payment.

The rest of the *onkwe honwe* of the Longhouse of One Family thought about what they should do. If they took up the weapons of war, they would be breaking the Great Peace; still, if they didn't do something, they might all come under the subjugation of the peoples they called *Atirontok*. It was the captured *Kenienké;haka* women who decided the issue.

Things remained the same for quite a few seasons. The *Kenienké:haka* men were continually made fun of for their weaknesses in hunting and the fact that women were such an authority in their councils.

One day a hunting party of *Atirontok* and *Kenienké:haka* were out hunting in the traditional manner with six men to each party. It had been a harsh winter, and there was little food to eat. For some reason the *Atirontok* spiritual leaders failed to find any game. It was decided the two hunting parties should split up.

The *Atirontok* had little success while hunting. Meanwhile, the *Kenienké:haka* hunters had come upon many caribou and had plenty to eat. When the two hunting parties met up, the *Kenienké:haka* showed the *Atirontok* their great success. The *Atirontok* became jealous and were afraid that they would be made fools of when they returned to the village. They decided that they would kill the *Kenienké:haka* hunting party and tell their peoples that they waited for *Kenienkeé:haka* but that they did not know what happened to them.

That evening as they slept, they clubbed the *Kenienké:haka* hunting party to death. When they arrived back at the main village on the island where the *Kenienké:haka* and the *Atirontok* lived, they carried back the meat that had been killed by the *Kenienké:haka and* said it was theirs.

Tekarihoken, the *royaner* of the village, asked the *Atirontok* hunters, "What happened to our men?"

They answered, "We don't know. We think they may have become lost somewhere. We tried to find them but could not."

Tekarihoken replied, "We will have to send out a search party to find out what has happened to them."

Not long after, the *Kenienké:haka* men went searching for their friends. They followed the *Atirontok* tracks back to where they had come from but could not find any evidence of their men.

As they were about to head back, one of the *Kenienké:haka* men said, "Look over there. It seems like something has been buried there."

The men began to dig out the snow. They then came upon the bodies of the six hunters and figured out what had happened. They returned to the village to tell *Tekarihoken* what they had found (Colden p. 4).

Immediately, *Tekarihoken* confronted the *Atirontok* war chief. "What did your men do to our men?" he asked.

The war chief yelled to his warriors, "Take these men and tie them up." *Tekarihoken* was now a hostage.

The Great Law had made the *Kenienké:haka* a peaceful peoples up to this time, and they were not known as fighters. However, they saw this as the last straw. For years they had asked *Teharonhia:wako* to help them, and now it was time to put their trust back in him.

One evening, the women decided that they had to do something. They held a council. The Clan mother of *Tekarihoken* said, "We have had enough. We have to break this bondage that we are under and release our men. Does anyone have an idea?"

A young woman stood up and said, "I have an idea. We will hold a feast and invite the *Atirontok* chiefs to come. Since we are in the maple syrup season, we will offer them some food. When they are seated, we will fling the hot maple syrup in their faces. The rest of us will release the prisoners. We will then make our escape by canoe. Instead of paddling on the south river that leads toward our brothers in the southern country, we will head west along the great river and turn down into *Oneota:haka* country. We have a better chance of escaping this way. We will need decoys to travel down the southern river to lead the *Atirontok* away from the elders and children."

The Clan mother said, "It sounds like a good plan."

The women boiled the syrup and prepared the feast. They invited the *Atirontok* chiefs, as planned, to the feast. When they arrived, the women sat them down and brought them their hot meal. As the women approached the war chiefs to offer them food, they flung the hot syrup that they were carrying into their faces (Morgan p. 5).

There was much commotion, and, as the *Atirontok* men rolled on the ground, the women stabbed them and clubbed them. Some of the elder men and young boys jumped *Tekarihoken's* guards and released him and the other men. They had hid their canoes near the lake at the west end of the river. They hoped that they would get away in time, before the *Atirontok* warriors could gather themselves and attack. A few of them headed east of the island to divert the warriors away from the rest.

As they paddled away, they were spotted by some of the *Atirontok* warriors who had heard the commotion. They yelled to the rest of their warriors that the *Kenienké:haka* were escaping to the lake that was at the head of the rapids. They got their war clubs, bows and arrows, and made their way to their canoes.

The *Kenienké:haka* had their children and elders with them; this slowed them up. The women meanwhile shared the paddling with the men. They decided that their only route of escape would be to travel down the great river as far as the first great lake, *Kanontario*, and head south, doubling back along the *Osweko* River to the southerly *Kenienké:haka* villages. They would then be in the heart of *Rotinonshonni* territory and would feel much safer. Even the *Atirontok* would not be foolish enough to follow them that far into *Rotinonshonni* territory.

As they traveled, they watched and hid during the day; then at night, they traveled down the great river toward the Great Lake. When they came to the Great Lake, they went south as far as the *Osweko* River. They began to travel down the *Osweko* and believed that they were safe. Suddenly one of the women pointed, "Look!"

The *Atirontok* war canoes were not far behind. It looked like they were going to be over-taken and killed by the *Atirontok* warriors.

Tekarihoken started to give the words of thanks. He yelled, "*Teharonhia:wako* and our grandfathers, help us."

Just then, out of the west, the sky began to darken, and the sounds of the grandfathers' thunders were heard. A storm hit the *Atirontok* canoes head-on, overturning them. Some of the *Atirontok* drowned, while the rest of the *Atirontok* warriors returned to their village (*Tehanetorens* pp 113–124).

The *Kenienké:haka* made their way back to safety, crossing at the *Oneota:haka* carrying place named Woods Creek, to the *Kenienké:haka* river. *Tekarihoken* settled into a village, naming it *Ossesneron*. The *Kenienké:haka* would later move across the river and call their village *Kahnawaké* - after the river rapids near the village they had left behind. The villages were west of the original village at Cohoes Falls and the village near the mountain divided by two rivers. That is how a Turtle Clan village ended up west of the Wolf Clan village at *Schoharie* Creek. Later on, there would come a time when another *Tekarihoken* and some of his peoples would return to their former village near the mountain divided between two rivers, naming it *Kahnawaké* once again.

It was not too many seasons after that the *Kenienké:haka* learned that more light-skinned men had landed and were now staying at the place where their old village was situated on the island near the mountain. These white men referred to themselves as French. They had befriended the *Atirontok*, who now resided there with the remaining captives who had not escaped with *Tekarihoken*.

One of these captives was *Iroquet*, now an *Atirontok* war leader. His people had blended in with the *Atirontok* and were known as the Little Nation. They lived near *Kanehsataké* along the Great River of the Algonquins (Grassman p. 61). Algonquin was a name given to the *Atirontok* by the French. *Iroquet* was one of the *Kenienké:haka* survivors adopted into the Martin clan of the *Atirontok* (Benton-Benai p. 96).

The *Kenienké:haka* wanted to remain at peace, in spite of all that had happened to them. After all, they had relations still living around the island, who had not escaped with them. They didn't want to have to go to war with their relative *Iroquet*.

One day, they heard that one of these light-skinned Frenchmen was coming down a river that led into their country with a group of *Atirontok*. They were not sure if they were coming for war or peace. The *Kenienké:haka* held a national council at Cohoes Falls to decide what to do.

The *royaner Ayenwatha* said, "Let us greet this man and befriend him. We will choose one *royaner* from each of our clans to head the delegation. We will meet him at the wood's edge, near the head of the lake that leads to the north country."

All the *royaner* agreed, and they chose *Ayenwatha*, *Shoskoharowane*, and *Teionhe:kon* to lead the delegation. They would all wear their ceremonial headdresses as befitted a special occasion.

The three *Kenienké:haka royaner*, one from each clan, camped out with their men not far from the *Atirontok* camp near the edge of the river at the shore of *Kaniaderiguarunte* Lake That Is The Gate To The Country (Lake Champlain). That night, the men called back and forth to each other between the two camps. They played their ceremonial drums to one another.

What the *Kenienké:haka* men didn't know was that the light-skinned man named Champlain had destructive weapons that they had never seen before. He planned to hide some of his men with their weapons under boats by the river.

The next day, the three *Kenienké:haka royaner* went out to meet the light-skinned man to say the three clear-minded words given by the first *Ayenwatha* and to wipe away any grief that might have occurred to them on the way. They wore their ceremonial headdresses as was befitting dignitaries. As they approached the clearing to greet the visitors, *Ayenwatha* held some wampum in his hands. He faced the light-skinned man and began to say, "We take away any pain that may have befallen you while on your journey here. We wipe away the tears from your eyes."

Suddenly the light-skinned man began to yell something. The men hidden under the boats suddenly sprang up with sticks that shot fire from them. Instantly, *Ayenwatha* and the other *royaner* fell to the ground. Soon, many others fell as well. The men ran in every direction in panic. They had never seen such thunderous power before coming from sticks that shot out fire and death. As they retreated, they tried to get their wounded, but it was to no avail. That day they lost fifty men, including their three *royaner*. This was devastating to the *Kenienké:haka*, as many had come from one village near Cohoes Falls (Biggar pp. 99–100). That same year, another light-skinned man sailed up a river that joined the *Tahnonatche* Between Two Mountains at the border of the country of the *Kenienké:haka* and *Mahican* near Cohoes Falls. The remaining *Kenienké:haka* were at first fearful of him (Richter p. 51).

The man got out of the ship and brought out one of the fire sticks. He said through a translator of the Wolf Peoples, the *Mahican*, "I have come here to trade with you. I will trade one of these fire sticks for fifty beaver skins."

The *Kenienké;haka royaner Tsha tekariwate* said to him, "This is quite excessive." However, *Tsha tekariwate* knew that they needed the fire sticks if they were going to defend their villages from the French.

That night, *Tsha tekariwate* held a council with the clan mothers and *royaner*.

He told them, "If we don't accept the fire sticks, we will be killed off by the *Atirontok* and their new friends."

The next day, *Tsha tekariwate* told the man. "This is what we agree to."

He then took out a wampum belt that *Ayenwatha* had made; it had two rows that ran down the middle of it.

He said to the light-skinned man, "You and your peoples represent one row, while my peoples and I another. We will live and trade, side by side one another. Neither of us will interfere with the affairs of the other, our way of life, beliefs and trade. This is the way it was set down by our forefathers whenever anyone enters into the Great Peace with us. You may rest here for a while, but don't stay too long." (Traditional Teachings, 1992, Great Law recital).

The light-skinned man agreed. These peoples were called Dutch, and their leaders would later be known as Corlear. This was because Corlear, a Dutch official, laughed one day when the *Kenienké:haka* placed tobacco to appease the water spirits of a lake. Corlear drowned that same day on the lake (Richter p. 24).

Not long after, the light-skinned Dutchmen brought out what looked to be water in a vessel. He said to a *Kenienké:haka* man, "Drink this, you will enjoy it."

The *Kenienké:haka* man took a drink; it burned when it went down his throat. Soon the man began to feel good, and he asked for more. In the future, the Dutch promised that they would bring more each time the *Kenienké:haka* came to trade at the trading post that they would set up.

When the Dutch set up their trading post, they placed Jacob Elkens at its head. He remained a friend of the *Kenienké:haka* until he was relieved (Richter p. 88). The Dutch traders learned that while under the influence of alcohol they could make the *Kenienké:haka* do what they wanted. Pretty soon, they were offering more and more alcohol to the *Kenienké-haka*. The effects were devastating; the *Kenienké:haka* began to be cheated by the Dutch, for they often didn't remember what they had done the night before. They then would return to the villages with alcohol and no other trading items. The women would hide out of fear of being beaten when this happened. The *Kenienké:haka* could do little about it because it was believed that a person who was out of his mind could not be judged in the same way as a person who was sane. Sometimes a murder would take place, and there would be forgiveness because the person was under the influence of the deadly spirit that lived in the drinking vessel that they called the mind changer.

In spite of this, there were important decisions that had to be made, and everyone had to be at their best. One of those decisions was, would they have to go on the war trail or would they try and remain at peace? They counseled with one another but could not come up with a final resolution. A few seasons later, the issue was decided not by the *Kenienke:haka* but by the keepers of the central fire, the *Onontaka:haka*.

The same light-skinned man, Champlain, who was French, attacked an *Onontaka:haka* village (Biggar, 1922–36, pp53–4). He had come by the same route that the *Kenienké:haka* had taken when they escaped from the *Atirontok* many seasons before. He laid siege to a village, killing the *royaner Rosehraha: hon* and many others. The Wendat, who were close cousins to the *Rotinonshonni,* had led him there. The *Wendat* now had guns and wanted war against them.

The Revival of the War Chiefs

A grand council was called *at Kanata kowa* village *in Onontaka:haka* territory. Representatives from all the Five Nations of the *Rotinonshonni* attended. The issue at hand was whether they should accept the weapons of war to defend themselves and possibly take the war trail once again. Most of the *royaner* had chosen peace. However, *Skanawati* was incensed at what had happened.

When it was his turn to speak, he said to the council, "It is time to change some of the things that occurred during the Great Peace. Things are not the same now since the coming of the light-skinned men, and perhaps it would be better if weapons were once again allowed to be taken up."

Many of the young men who stood behind their *royaner* nodded their heads in agreement. Even some of the Clan matrons who had suffered from the attack by the Frenchmen agreed.

Skanawati said, "I want revenge for *Rosehraha: hon.* My Clan mother is willing to allow me to carry the name of *Rosehraha: hon*, Axe Handler, when I go to war. This will appease *Rosehraha: hon's* spirit." (Jacob Thomas 1992, Great Law recital)

As *Skanawatis'* resolution was brought up in the council, *Tekarihoken* stood up and said, "I agree with *Skanawati*. Things have to change or we will be all killed."

What had really brought the issue to the forefront was an attack by the *Wendat* on the main *Oneota:haka* village. So devastating was the attack that the *Oneota:haka* Clan matrons had to plead to the *Kenienke-haka* clans for men to replace their losses (Grassman p. 105)

When it was the *Oneota:haka's* turn to speak, *Rotatshe:té* said, "We have lost too many of our men because of the fire sticks that the French give to the Wendat. I agree. I am ready to take the path of war."

There was confusion in the confederacy council, for the older *royaner* knew that they were losing support to the younger generation, many of whom wanted revenge. The younger generation agreed with *Tekarihoken,*

Rotatshe:té and *Skanawatis'* position. The council wanted to prevent a division from taking place in the council and the communities. They knew that they could not prevent individuals from going to war.

Tatotaho stood up and said, "We have decided that, if *Skanawati* goes to war, he would have to take off his title of *royaner*. When he returns, he may retain his title. There will also be a new type of representative of the peoples who will be selected by the clans. This is so that some of the younger generation can sit in council, and we may hear their voice. His title will be based solely on merit. They will be called a Pine Tree Chief. There will also be a war chief who will stand behind the *royaner* to represent himself on behalf of the warriors. We must make sure what happened to the three *Kenienké:haka royaner* does not happen again. From now on, we will send our war chiefs to speak for us. They are more able to defend themselves than we are." (Morgan p. 99)

This resolution seemed to appease the younger members of the council and the young men who backed them. It seemed like they were now being sanctioned to go to war. The *Kaokwa:haka* were the most opposed to the new resolutions.

Teiohonwe:thon stood up and said, "This goes against the Great Law of Peace. I want to make a resolution that these new ideas remain separate from the Great Law of Peace. They should be called *Skanawatis'* Laws of War. This is so there will be no confusion in the teachings of the Great Peace. These teachings will govern the responsibilities of those who go to war and not those of the *royaner*." (Parker p. 52)

Teiohonwe:thon's resolution went around the council, and everyone agreed. The *Kaokwa haka*, however, lived further west than the others and were not as exposed to the dangers as the others were. They also had the powerful *Sonontowa haka* next to them at the western door.

The *Sonontowa:haka* had heard rumours that the light-skinned Frenchmen had traveled as far west as their country and were making arrangements with nations living west of them. They were also becoming fearful.

Skaniatar:io stood up, "If we are the keepers of the western door, we will need all the help we can get. The Sonontowa:haka agree that something has to be done. We accept the changes."

Conciliation with one another was the most important thing to occur if the confederacy was to survive. Cracks were already starting to occur within its structure. What they didn't know was that something so devastating would occur to all of them that it would shake their belief in *Teharonhia:wako,* as well as the very foundations of the confederacy.

It was not long after that many of the *onkwe honwe* began to fall ill. Their faces and bodies would boil and blister, and they would then succumb to its effects.

The worse hit was the *Kenienké:haka* and the *Oneota:haka*. They began to lose many of their elders who were the most knowledgeable in the culture, as well as the young who would be the ones who would learn from them. This left a great void in the spiritual beliefs in their cultures. It seemed like every day there were other condolences taking place and more losses. The strain of all that was happening was becoming too much to take.

To replace their losses and appease the grieving Clan matrons, the *Kenienké:haka* men started going out in war parties to capture enemy men. They were adopted into their villages to replace losses and to calm the grieving mothers and widows. The other nations began to follow suit. In time, it seemed like there were more adopted and captives living in the villages than there were original members of the village. Instead of people following the roots of the tree to its source, they were now being forcefully absorbed as members (Trigger pp. 242–251).

Some of the adoptees were *Wendat* who had already been exposed to the new religion called Christianity. They had asked that they continue to be allowed to practice their new religion even after being held captive. There were also traditional *Wendat* who volunteered to join who were incensed at the French Black Robes and who would only trade with the *Wendat* who had become Christian.

Name: _____   Time: _____

Learning Activity

1. Make a list of the Indigenous names and their meanings. Compare them to the names in use today. What are some other Indigenous names you can find along the St. Lawrence and Ottawa Rivers?

2. Read Samuel De Champlain's Journal of his battle with the Mohawk peoples in 1609. Compare his version with the story you read in this section?

3. Discuss how history can be taught by using various viewpoints?

4. What were the Mohawk peoples like that you were taught about in school? Do you view them differently after reading this section?

Review

1. Warfare has existed among all peoples including Indigenous peoples as well as European peoples. In the short section you have read there are many battles that have taken place. Why have the Mohawk and their Iroquois allies been depicted as more warlike than other Indigenous and non-Indigenous peoples in Canadian history?

2. In reading this text, look at the conflicts between Indigenous peoples before the arrival of Europeans. How did these conflicts affect the decisions of the different Indigenous groups in deciding how they would react to the arrival of the newcomers, and which newcomers they would side with?

References

Benton-Benai, E. (1988). The Mishomis book: *the voice of the Ojibwa*. St. Paul, Minnesota: Red School House.

Biggar, H. P. (1922–36). The Works of Samuel De Champlain: *reprinted, translated and annotated by six canadian scholars under the general editorship of H.P. Biggar*. Toronto, Ontario: Champlain Society.

Grassman, Tom. (1969). *The Mohawk Indians and their valley: being a chronology documentary record to the end of 1963.* Schenectady, NY: Hugo Photography and Printing Co.

Kelsey, Isabel. (1984). Joseph Brant 1743–1807: *man of two worlds*. Syracuse New York: Syracuse University Press.

Morgan, Louis Henry. (1962). League of the Iroquois. New York: Citadel Press.

Parker, Arthur C. (1989). *Seneca myths and folk tales*. Lincoln, Nebraska: University of Nebraska Press

Rice, Brian .(2013). The Rotinonshonni: A Traditional Iroquoian History Through the Eyes of Teharonhia:wako and Sawiskera. pp. 251–265.

Syracuse New York: Syracuse University Press.

Richter, Daniel (1992). *The ordeal of the longhouse: the people of the Iroquois and their neighbours in Indian North America 1600–1800*. Syracuse, New York: Syracuse University Press.

Shea, J. G. (1870). History and General Description of New France *by Rev. P.F.X. De Charlevois, S.J.: Loyola.* Chicago, Illinois: University Press.

Smaltz, Peter. (1991). *The Ojibwa of southern Ontario*. Toronto: University of Toronto Press.

Tehanetorens (1992). *Tales of the Iroquois volumes 1 and 11*. Ohseweken, Ontario: Iroqrafts Ltd.

Thomas, Jacob. (1992) *Traditional Teachings*. Iroquois Institute, Sept 19–27, Ohseweken, Ontario

Thomas, Jacob. (1992). *The Great Law of Peace*, Nine day oral recital, Sept 19-27, The Iroquois Institute.

Thomas, Jacob. (1994). *The Great Law of Peace,* Twelve Day Oral Recital, June 26–27, Ohseweken, Ontario.

Trigger, Bruce. (1989). *Natives and newcomers: Canada's heroic age reconsidered*. Montreal, Quebec & Kingston, Ontario: McGill-Queens University Press.

Warren, William. (1984). *History of the Ojibwa people*. Minnesota: Historical Society.

Whitehead, Ruth. (1991). *The old man told us: excerpts from Micmac history, 1500–1950*. Halifax, Nova Scotia: Nimbus Publishing.

Coldon, Cadwallader. (1980). *The history of the Five Nations: depending on the provinces of New York in America.* New York: Cornell University Press.

MORE ENCOUNTERS BETWEEN INDIGENOUS PEOPLES AND NEWCOMERS IN EASTERN CANADA: NO LONGER ALLIES BUT SUBJECTS/WARDS OF THE CROWN

Introduction

This section will include both British North American and Canadian government policies towards Indigenous peoples living in Canada. The preliminary will begin with a brief history of British North America in the nineteenth century leading up to the formation of Canada. The second part of the section will deal specifically with government policies up to the 1876 Indian Act as cited in a special report called 'The Historical Development of the Indian Act' written in part by Mohawk activist *Kahn-Tineta Horn*. In later editions, *Kahn-Tineta* had been written from the record as a contributor to the work due to her participation in the Oka Crisis of 1990 while working for the Department of Indian Affairs. I was only happy to send her a copy that acknowledges her important contribution. It is important to note that the interpretation of policies and motivations of government are mine. I have only referenced the policies. I also have used the term Indian for First Nations because the term is entrenched in government policies and in this case doesn't apply to Métis and Inuit.

Preliminary

Allies and Pre-Confederation Treaty Making

After the War of 1812 had ended, the English authorities of British North America had retained control over most of the Maritimes including Nova Scotia, New Brunswick, Cape Breton Island and Prince Edward Island as well as Upper and Lower Canada, later named Ontario and Quebec. The borders between British North America and the United States of America had remained intact much as before the war. Many of the Indigenous peoples living along the United States side of the border had lost their lands as a result of joining the British in the war. Some of them would continue to fight the Americans as they were driven further west. Others remained inside the border of British North America, taking a chance that they would be treated better.

   Those who lived in the Maritimes and Upper and Lower Canada would see the British give their best lands away to English loyalists as had occurred during the previous war between British North America and the United States. Sometimes these people were referred to as early and late loyalists depending when they arrived. The most affected would be the *Mi'kmaq* of New Brunswick, Cape Breton Island, and Nova Scotia and the *Ojibwa* Roasted Words (shortened dialect) of Upper Canada. As a result of settlers encroaching on their land, they would suffer from starvation as a result of over hunting by loyalists and others (Paul p. 184).

Much like other Indigenous peoples who had been displaced from their homelands, they would be forced onto marginal lands with the least value. As their way of life disappeared, some would turn to alcohol. New diseases struck their villages. This was a hard time for most Indigenous peoples living in the east. Those situated west of Upper Canada were still free to practice their traditions such as the Sundance. In the east, many traditions had already started to fall by the wayside, as the traditional hunting way of life became lost.

It was during this period that the first treaties for land were signed between the Crown and the *Ojibwa* in Upper Canada. The *Mi'kmaq* had already signed treaties with the Crown in 1725, 1752 and 1760 called Peace and Friendship treaties, but not for land. These Peace and Friendship treaties were based on the idea that the *Mi'kmaq* would not harm the English and in return truck houses were to be built. These truck houses would be small trading stations where the *Mi'kmaq* could trade their furs for income and supplies (Paul p. 115–117.)

During the wars between the French and English, the *Mi'kmaq* often sided with the French. The French seemed to respect the *Mi'kmaq* more than the English. The English would break most of the agreements they had made with the *Mi'kmaq* which created deep resentment. By the time of the Seven Years War, sometimes called the French and Indian war, the *Mi'kmaq* became involved in more conflicts with the English that would have devastating consequences. After signing another Peace and Friendship treaty with the English, the *Mi'kmaq* would not only suffer the consequences of losing their lands but their independence as well.

Much the same thing would occur to the *Ojibwa* of Upper Canada. After the English became victorious over the French in 1760, the *Ojibwa* who had been allies of the French then gave their loyalty to the British Crown. In order to keep the peace the English made promises to the *Ojibwa* that they would continue to trade with them much as the French had done. This included providing them with gifts in exchange for inhabiting their lands.

Under the leadership of *Pontiac,* an *Ojibwa-Odawa Ogemaw* Chief, many Indigenous peoples living along the Great Lakes region aligned to fight against the English. This happened because they were not being supplied provisions and were being restricted from trading with whom they wanted by the English, as they had been promised. *Pontiac* and those allied with him won several major victories over the English before many of them succumbed to a smallpox epidemic as a result of being given infected blankets by the English (Dowd p. 190).

Although *Pontiac* didn't win the war, they were able to force a concession from the British Crown. It was called the Royal Proclamation of 1763 and was signed by King George III. As mentioned in a previous section, it affirmed some rights of Indigenous peoples to the lands west of the Appalachian Mountains. However, it negated the full sovereign rights that they had previously by making the Crown the sole future beneficiary of Indigenous lands (Dowd p. 177).

By the time the two wars were over between the British and the Americans, the displacement of the *Ojibwa* from their homelands in Upper Canada had begun. The British Crown would begin the process of signing a series of treaties with individual *Ojibwa* bands for land. One of the treaties was called the Gunshot Treaty signed between an *Ojibwa* chief and Captain Crawford in 1783. The reason it was called the Gunshot Treaty was because somewhere near York (now Toronto), Captain Crawford shot a gun in the air and told the *Ojibwa* chief that he would claim the land as far as the sound of a gunshot. This treaty was disputed many years later when no one could figure out how far a gunshot could sound (Shmaltz p. 126).

Another treaty, called the Chenail Ecarté, was signed just before the War of 1812, between the *Ojibwa* and the English around Lake St. Clair, when the *Ojibwa* were given a paper to sign so that they could receive guns to fight with the English against the Americans. They were also told that if they signed their rights to their lands to the Crown their interests in the lands would be protected. Once the war was over, upon returning home they were shown the piece of paper and told they had signed away their land (p. 125).

Sometimes individual chiefs like Yellowhead, living around the Lake Simcoe region north of York, would sign away land that was not theirs (p. 128). He probably thought he would receive personal benefits that were promised by the British North American Government, so what would he have to lose by signing?

In any case, both the *Ojibwa* and *Mi'kmaq* were no longer militarily powerful; therefore, it was easier to either push them off their land, or in the case of the *Ojibwa* sign papers without understanding the meaning. After all, most could not read or write. And, in some cases there were chiefs who didn't care. It would be during these fateful years that the British Crown would be begin to create legislation that would affect the rights of not only the *Ojibwa* and *Mi'kmaq* , but other Indigenous peoples as well.

It was during this time when the *Ojibwa* of central and western Canada would lose their most important lands, the *Saugeen* Open Water (from Wasaga Beach to the Bruce Penninsula). In 1840 Upper and Lower Canada became referred to as Canada West and Canada East. Years before, on the shores of Lake Huron, named after the French designation for the *Wendat,* from the French word hure (because of the style of their hair), the *Ojibwa* won their greatest victory over their rivals to the south, the *Rotinonshonni* Longhouse Peoples (Iroquois). They had been led by leaders from the *Kamick Dodem* Fish Clan and solidified their control over the territory. The place would be called *Nottowasaga* Beach shortened later to *Wasaga or* (Snake) Iroquois Beach. Now they were about to lose control of this last pristine area.

In spite of the English vow to protect their remaining lands from encroachment by white settlers, the English did nothing when white settlers began squatting in the *Saugeen*. Instead, British North American government officials began the process of more treaty making. This would result in the *Ojibwa* moving onto reserves. By 1840 there had been a push to have all *Ojibwa* of Canada West be moved and resettled onto *Manitoulin* Island Great Spirit Island. In 1836, the English had already negotiated a deal with fourteen *Odawa* leaders (Trading Peoples) to allow *Ojibwa* to move onto the western portion of the island while preserving the east for the *Odawa*. They also set up an Anglican Protestant mission at *Manitowaning* Place of Spirits to counter the Roman Catholic mission at *Wikwemikong* Bay Of The Beaver.

The English, now having control of the western part of Manitoulin Island, began to negotiate with the *Ojibwa* newcomers, as they wanted it opened up for white settlement. By 1862, *Ojibwa* chiefs were given double the money if they signed treaties to move onto reserves. It was a convenient way of getting possession of Indigenous lands by bringing in other Indigenous peoples and negotiating with them instead. (Morse pp. 210–213) The *Odawa* refused to sign anymore agreements involving their territory and to this day refer to the eastern part of Manitoulin Island as being unceeded.

Prior to this, an incident had occurred at the head of Lake Huron at *Bawating* Place of the Rapids later called Sault St. Marie by French traders. The area had been close to the original home of the *Mississauga* Big Water Outlet *Ojibwa,* some of whom had migrated down towards the *Saugeen* Lake People years before and had fought the *Rotinonshonni*. A group of about 150 *Ojibwa* and *Metis* had stopped mining production at Bruce Mines by *Mica Bay* just east of *Bawating*. In the lead was a young *Ojibwa-Metis* named *Shingwauk* Little Pine Tree (Chute p. 132). It resulted in the British North American Government deciding that they had better negotiate treaties with the *Ojibwa* that included the central-northern regions of Canada West.

The Government developed a new type of treaty to be signed. Instead of negotiating with individual *Ojibwa* bands as was done further south, they would have one treaty written up and then invite representatives of as many *Ojibwa* bands in the area as possible to sign the treaty. In the year 1850 William Robinson would be sent to Sault St. Marie to administer the signing of the treaties. He negotiated two treaties, taking in the northern area of Lake Huron and *Kitchi Gami* Lake Superior.

Robinson promised the *Ojibwa* that they would always be able to maintain their way of life as long as it didn't infringe on mining activity or settlements, of which he promised there would be few. The *Ojibwa* would also receive yearly payments from the government with the value increasing in accordance with the wealth of the land. He also promised the Metis who were involved during the *Mica Bay* incident that their rights to hunting and land would be taken care of.

The promises to the Metis were never kept and when treaty was signed with the Ojibwa chiefs, Robinson told them to take which Metis they wanted and incorporate them into their bands and then discard the rest (Chute pp. 142–143). Because *Shingwauk* considered himself Ojibwa even though his father was white, it didn't affect him. This would begin a more than 150 year struggle for the Metis to affirm their rights within the future Province of Ontario. The Robinson Huron and Robinson Superior Treaties would be the model used for all subsequent number treaties out west.

Pre-confederation Wards

In 1840, as the provinces of Upper and Lower Canada were officially united to form the one province of Canada called Canada East and Canada West, a question was put forward by government officials. What should be done about the Indigenous peoples living in the province and the lands they lived upon? A commission was set up in 1844 called the Bagot Commission with evidence given by missionaries, Indian agents and superintendents. It was decided that Indigenous peoples would no longer be considered as allies but rather as wards of the British Crown. This meant they were to be treated like children rather than as adults, with the British Crown as their guardian. (Horn and Lerch p. 14)

Since they were not to be considered adults they would have to be treated differently than British subjects in Canada. They would first have to be set apart on reserves and then taught how to become adults. This meant that they would no longer have large expanses of land to live on to practice their traditions. The first thing that would have to happen is their spiritual leaders, elders, and traditions would have to be replaced by Christian missionaries and the Christian religion. The way to achieve this was by separating the children from their influence and, even if necessary, from their parents.

One of the first acts of legislation by the Parliament of the Province of Canada was called the Indian Protection and Civilization Act. (p. 23) It was said to be conceived to protect the lands of Indigenous peoples from white interlopers who might try and trick them out of their lands. In reality, it reinforced the British Crown's guardianship over Indigenous peoples by allowing it to retain the exclusive right to acquire Indigenous lands. Because of the Royal Proclamation of 1763, even though all land Indigenous peoples lived on was considered Crown land, the Crown still had to negotiate with them for their lands. This reinforced the Crown's position. The fear was that Americans might try and acquire Indigenous lands in Canada. This was in line with the Royal Proclamation of 1763 that allowed an Indigenous usufruct but not ownership.

Once treaties were signed, Indigenous peoples who were signatories had to move onto reserves where they would be registered and under the watchful eye of an Indian Agent appointed by the Crown. Many Indigenous peoples refused to move off of their hunting grounds and were subsequently referred to as squatters by the Crown, thus given no rights. This was the beginning of Indigenous peoples being designated under different categories such as status, treaty, or non-status Indians. Non-status Indians are those who didn't get registered while status and treaty Indians are those who did. The protection policies were there to protect the interests of the British Crown and not to protect the interests of Indigenous peoples.

When outsiders begin to make decisions about membership in another's society, the result is a loss of that societies' control over its destiny. By the 1850's, the Province of Canada was making the decisions as to who was or wasn't an Indian.

By 1857, the government of Canada began developing other policies for Indigenous peoples that would infringe on their rights. These were called the 'Enfranchisement Acts' better known as the 'Acts for the Gradual Civilization of the Indian Tribes'. (p. 28) Enfranchisement meant that you could lose your rights as a member of your own society in favour of another.

With enfranchisement, it was decided that any male Indian person who received a formal education would lose any rights as an Indian. This would also include his wife and children. It also meant that if an Indian woman married a non-Indian, she and her children would no longer be considered Indian. (p. 27) This angered many First Nation leaders and so they protested. They felt no one should be able to decide if they were Indian or not. These leaders held a meeting at Six Nations reserve in order to find out how to stop the government.

It seemed after fighting to help save British North America from the Americans the government was trying to legislate them out of existence.

The government decided to create different policies for Indians living in the west from those in the east. They felt that Indians in the Province of Canada were more civilized than those living in the west; therefore, the policies would have to be more stringent. Indians in the prairies and beyond were still living a traditional life by hunting buffalo and other wildlife for their subsistence, and it was felt that drastic action was needed for this to change.

Although most traditional Indigenous groups had defined territories, land was something to be shared and not owned. One could not put a price on something that had been given as a gift for human beings to live upon by the Creator. It was important to the government that this worldview be changed in order for to acquire Indian lands. More treaties would be required. In order for this to occur, Indigenous peoples would first need to be converted to Christianity, a religion that had no spiritual relationship to the land. It was always easier to get Indigenous leaders to sign a treaty once they had been converted. By 1860, the Province of Canada East and West was on its way to becoming a new country. More land would be needed to provide for the influx of new immigrants, and Indigenous peoples out west had lots of it.

Part of the problem for the government was that Indigenous peoples were not assimilating fast enough in the east, so how were they going to assimilate those still living a traditional life out west? The Manitoulin experiment of separating Indians from their mainland homelands and sequestering them on Manitoulin Island was not helping them assimilate. A committee called the Pennefather, Talford, and Worthington Commission was sent to find out why they were not being assimilated. They reported back, "With sorrow however we must confess that any hopes of raising the Indians as a body to the social or political level of their white neighbours is yet a glimmer and distant spark." (Horn and Lerch p. 30)

What they didn't take into account was that most Indigenous peoples felt their way of life was superior to the white man's way of life and didn't feel a need to change. It was true that the white man had invented many things; however, it was perceived by Indigenous peoples that this made him both inefficient and incapable of taking care of himself. With all of the broken promises the white man made, it appeared that he also lacked values as well often going back on his word.

For most Indigenous peoples, the white man's way of life had created listless people who relied on technology to do their work. Could a white person make his own transportation, clothes, and weapons many Indigenous leaders would ask themselves throughout the years? At the same time, the white man didn't believe that an Indigenous person could survive in his world as an Indian.

Post-Confederation Wards

By 1867, British North America turned over jurisdiction to the newly formed Federal Government of the country called Canada, along with the authority to legislate all matters concerning Indians and their lands within section 91 sub-section 24 of the British North America Act. The following year, Parliament passed an act giving the Superintendent – General of Indian Affairs control over the management of Indian lands. This included any moneys that came from the resources such as timber from those lands.

This was overturned in 1888, during the St. Catherine's Millings Court Case; whereupon, the Provincial Government of Ontario took the Federal Government of Canada to court over jurisdiction of resources on lands signed over in treaties. The province won the decision by using section 88 of the British North America Act, signifying that resources belonged under the jurisdiction of the province. Indigenous peoples, who signed Treaty Three in 1873, had no say in the decisions regarding the lands and resources in question (Morse p. 98). Once again they were said by the courts, to have had only a usufructuary right to their lands (to hunt and fish). This included even the time before the treaty was signed, with the Crown having the greater authority even before acquiring the lands, and the province reaping the benefits from its wealth.

By1869, the full impact of enfranchisement came into effect as Indigenous women began losing their rights as Indians under the law, along with the rights of their children, if they married a white man. On the other hand, a white woman who married an Indian man became an Indian under the legislation. (p. 54) As mentioned, the purpose for the legislation had it beginnings in Pre-Confederation Canada and was a result of the Indigenous population increasing rather than decreasing. The idea that Indigenous peoples belonged to a vanishing race was not taking hold fast enough for the government; therefore, it was going to accelerate the process.

By the 1870's, John A. Macdonald, Canada's first Prime Minister decided that it was time to open up the remaining lands in Ontario and further west, to white settlement. He began the process of removing Indian children from their homes to be segregated from their parents and institutionalized, where they could be indoctrinated into the Christian belief system and eventually mainstream society. In 1879, he sent Nicholas Flood Davin to the United States to report on the Industrial School system there. They had been set up by President Ulysses S. Grant as a policy called aggressive civilization. Davin discovered that they were administered by Indian agencies in collaboration with various Church organizations. Davin reported back that in order civilize the Indians they had to "take away their simple mythology." This would be done by the churches through what he thought were the superior morals and values of Christianity (Miller pp. 101–2).

Eventually, with $44,000 three schools were built, the first two being Catholic at Qu'Appelle and High River Alberta, and the third Anglican, at Battleford, Saskatchewan. The three locations chosen had been prime areas where Indigenous peoples either had deep cultural ties or had been in conflict with the Federal government while protecting their rights to their lands (p. 103). After 1876, with the consolidation of Federal Government policies towards Indigenous peoples in Canada into the 'Indian Act', the most stringent policies towards Indigenous peoples would occur through the 1976 Indian Act and with the help of the Residential Boarding Schools, the dismantling of Indigenous cultures, languages and governance

In 1869, the Federal Government began the process of dismantling traditional governing structures in favour of an electoral process that it would have ultimate control over. This was a response to those traditional chiefs who were organizing against enfranchisement. The Superintendent of Indian Affairs gave himself the power to depose any elected chief based on their morality or lack thereof. (p. 65) In other words traditional leaders were deemed immoral as opposed to Christian leaders who were of good moral standing. Women were excluded from being elected from leadership positions or from voting for leaders because at the time only men were allowed to vote in Canada.

By 1880 a new department was created, Department of Indian Affairs, exclusively for Indians, dealing a final blow to any chance of remaining self-governing. Métis would be excluded from the legislation and would end up with even less chances of self-sufficiency than Indians.

Learning Activity

1. Look up and read the Peace and Friendship treaties of 1725 and 1752 in the Maritimes. Are Indigenous rights included in them?

2. Look up the Robinson Huron and Superior treaties. Did the Ojibwa receive everything that was promised them in the treaties?

3. Find out how the Metis of Ontario have fared since the signing of the Robinson Huron and Superior treaties?

4. In reading from the text about the early policies of British North American and later Canadian governments what are your conclusions about them?

Review

1. What is a usufructuary right? Are there any other examples of a usufructuary right in Canada that you can find?

2. What are some of the main Government policies towards Indigenous peoples in the text?

3. What does it mean when we say pre-confederation treaties?

4. Who has jurisdiction over Indigenous peoples in Canada? Who has jurisdiction over lands and resources where Indigenous peoples live?

References

Chute, Janet. (1998). The Legacy of Shingwaukonce: *a century of Native leadership.* Toronto, Buffalo, London: University of Toronto Press.

Dowd, Gregory. (2002). War and heaven: *Pontiac, the Indian nations & the British. Empire.* Baltimore & London: John Hopkins University Press.

Miller, J.R. (1996). Shingwauk's vision*: a history of Native residential schools*. Toronto, Buffalo, London: University of Toronto Press.

Morse, Barry. (1989). Indigenous People and the law. Ottawa: Carleton University Press

Paul, Daniel. (1993). We Were not the Savages*: a Micmac perspective on the collision of European and Indigenous civilization*. Halifax: Nimbus Publishing.

Treaties and Historical Research Centre, P.R.E. Group, Indian and Northern Affairs. (1978). *The historical development of the Indian Act* : Ottawa Ontario.

Schmaltz, Peter. (1991). The Ojibwa of Southern Ontario. Toronto, Buffalo, London: University of Toronto Press.

ENCOUNTERS BETWEEN INDIGENOUS PEOPLES AND NEWCOMERS FROM THE EAST TO CENTRAL CANADA: FURS, METIS, AND NORTHERN CREE

Introduction

In this section of the text, we will look at the development of the fur trade from both northern and eastern Canada to the mid-west. Also, how two rival fur trading companies would not only be influential in opening up the west to settlement, but through the union of European and some Indigenous men involved in the fur trade from the east, and Indigenous women from the mid-west, would help to propagate a new Indigenous Nation: the *Métis* Nation. We will end this chapter with the fur trade and the *Métis* Nation in Manitoba. In the text, I have made a distinction between Metis, or those descended from simply Euro-British and Canadian men mostly Scotts and Indian woman and their counterparts *Métis*, a unique society resulting from unions between Frenchmen and Indian women who nationalized in the Red River region of Manitoba.

Preliminary

The Fur Trade

As early as 1642 Ville Marie (Montreal) had become the main center of the fur trade. As we have already read Algonquian peoples and the *Wendat* were indispensable to the French as trading partners. Travelling along the same northerly artic route as Henry Hudson years before, the English set up a trading post on what became known as Hudson Bay. In 1670 King Charles II gave a Royal Charter to the Company of Adventurers of England. It would soon be called the Hudson's Bay Company. They would have the exclusive right to trade with the Indigenous peoples in what became known as Ruperts Land (Brizinski p. 80). The Hudson's Bay Company was to develop trading relationships with the northerly Algonquian peoples who referred to themselves as *Illinew* or *Eeyou* The People. These people also had an ancient name for themselves which was in north *Kristineau* Human/ Spirit; in the south *Kinistineau*; and in the west *Kilistineau*. It is from *Kristineau* that we have the name that was given collectively to all, Cree. The most northerly Cree referred to their area as *Whapmagoostui* Place of the Beluga. In even more northerly regions lived the Inuit. However, the Inuit traditional life would not be affected by contact until years later.

Cree elders still say that before the coming of the Europeans, their *Miteo* Shamans knew that the European was coming as they had dreams about the event that would change their lives forever. They just didn't know when and where it would occur. In fact the Cree elder Louis Bird (Personal Correspondence: 2001) tells a story about a *Miteo* seeing bearded men floating towards them on an island. This is a similar story to that of the *Mi'kmaq*.

It was during this period that those who the Cree referred to as *Atoway* Snakes (Iroquois) would send war parties to their region and the *Miteo* would use their powers to thwart them. After receiving the gun a *Miteo* was said to have placed it on a bipod facing a path that the *Atoway* were traveling. Using the power of *Binisè* Thunder Bird (lightning) he was able to discharge an electrical bolt through the gun that destroyed the war party. (Bird 2001: Personal Correspondence).

There is another story that one of the Cree was captured and was adopted among the *Atoway*. One day he was taken along a trail that went far into the south where it was warm. There he witnessed strange looking animals, one of which looked like a frog with large mouth and long tail (Alligator). After escaping the *Atoway*, he told his people this story and many more adventures that he had (Bird 2001: Personal Correspondence). There is a good chance that the Cree prisoner was adopted by the *Kenienké:haka* who had a trail that ran from their country deep into the far south.

In the Hudson Bay region, as a result of the union between English and Scottish traders and Cree and *Dené* women, a distinct society started to evolve, sometimes referred to as half-breeds and sometimes as country born. Later on, some would mix with another group similar to them, the *Métis* further south, while others would remain as a distinct group among themselves or later be referred to as Metis. These Metis/*Métis* would be important intermediaries between Indigenous peoples in the south and those in the north. As they married, names such as Mackay would be passed down among the Cree from generation to generation.

Hudson Bay was an important meeting point for the rivers that converged from the *Kichisippi* Great River (Ottawa) flowing north from the Mattawa Meeting Place to the rivers that flowed from *Manitopai* Where The Creator Rested (Lake Manitoba) that flowed north. The *Nakota* The People (Assiniboine); the *Kristineau* (Cree) and later the *Anishnaabe* (Saulteaux) would all use these river routes to trade at the Bay.

As we have read in other sections, wars between the English and the French had affected the lives of many Indigenous peoples in the North East. However, there was another type of battle that took place besides physical confrontation and that was economic. Once the Hudson's Bay Company was established, it gave a monopoly for trade in the north to English traders from Great Britain many from the Orkney Islands.

This resulted in a trade war between the French traders who were traveling along the *Kichisippi* Great River (Ottawa River) into the interior and the English traders who had established themselves at the Bay. The French under the command of De Troyes (Detroit) had tried to secure the bay from the English understanding its strategic importance. He had used the *Anishnaabe* (Algonquin) who lived along the *Kichisippi* Great River (Ottawa River) as his guides (Pain p. 28). For several years the Bay passed hands between the two rivals but the French were finally thwarted in 1713 (Brizinski p. 80). The great advantage of trading from the Bay was that the trading vessels could port there; whereas, the French had to travel great distances by canoe portaging the frequent rough waters of a chain of rivers that led into the interior.

The advantage that the French had over the English was the good relations they had with their Indigenous allies. From the very beginning of trade between the people of New France and the Indigenous peoples they encountered, the French were willing to send their young men to learn the languages and customs of the Indigenous peoples. From the *Courier de Bois* Runners Of The Woods to the later *Voyagers* of the North West Company, Frenchmen traveled, lived, and intermarried with Indigenous women. Some of them would be the forefathers of a new society of Indigenous people that would spring up out of the unions between these voyagers and the Indigenous women in the mid-west: the *Métis* Nation.

In 1738, A French explorer named Pierre Gaultier de La Vèrendrye was one of the first French explorers to visit the junction of two rivers and build a small trading post. Fighting between Indigenous people in the area and the loss of a son the previous year resulted in de La Vérendrye traveling further west (Milloy p. 43). The Cree called one river the *Miscousipi* Red River and the other became known as the *Assinipouian* by the *Anishnaabe* (Saulteaux). The junction between the two rivers was called La Forche 'the forks' by the French traders. The original people who inhabited the area, the *Nakota* The People were named *Assiniboine* Rock Boilers and were given that name by the Cree who lived north of them and the *Anishnaabe* (Saulteaux) whom they had traded with. The fur traders would refer to the *Assiniboine* simply as Sioux, an abbreviation from the suffix of the word *Nadowaysis* Little Snakes. Eventually the *Assiniboine* would move west as they were displaced by the *Anishnaabe* (Saulteaux). The name given by the Cree for the location of the two rivers was *Winippi* Muddy Waters (Winnipeg). Men like La Vèrendrye were influential in developing the much needed trading relationships between the French and Indigenous peoples out west. *Winippi* was a strategic location for them because by establishing a trading post there they could control the trade to the Bay.

Much has been written about the evolution of the Métis Nation as a result of those unions between the French traders who had established themselves around *Winippi* and Indigenous women they married. However, Frenchmen were not the only ones to travel west and intermarry with *Cree and Ojibwa* women and begin the propagation of the *Métis* Nation.

After the English had defeated the French in 1760, they needed to secure a peace with the Indigenous allies of the French living in the area of Montreal. These were mostly *Kenienké:haka* People Of The Flint (Mohawk) who had arrived from the south around 1670, and had accepted the Roman Catholic religion as their faith. They lived in communities that also included, *Anishnaabe* First Humans (Algonquins), *Wendat* Islanders, *Abenaki* People Of The Dawn Light, Nipissing *Anishnaabe* First Humans (Ojibwas). In fact, during the wars between the English and French, seven of these communities had united and formed the Seven Nations Confederacy siding with the French against the English in their wars.

This was a result of a dispute in the 1680's between members of the *Rotinonshonni* Longhouse People (Iroquois Confederacy) and one of the member nations the *Kenienké:haka* Flint People (Mohawk) who had moved back to *Tiotiake* Where The People Split (Montreal) into the communities of *Kahnawaké* The Place Of The Rapids and *Kanehsatake* Place Of The Sand Banks. The central nation of the *Rotinonshonni* Longhouse People (Iroquois) the *Onontaka:haka* People of the Mountains had tried to kick the *Kenienké:haka* of these two communities out of the *Rotinonshonni* Confederacy because some of them had been coerced by the French under the command of a French General named Dennonville to help them raid the *Sonontowa: haka* People Of The Great Hill (Seneca).

This left a bitter taste in the mouths of all parties involved, with the result that the *Kenienké:haka* near *Tiotaké* established a new confederacy with the Algonquian peoples in the area. This confederacy was formidable and with the two communities established at the head of the *Kaniatarowanenneh* River of the Longhouse People (St. Lawrence River) and the *Kichisippi* Great River (Ottawa), they provided a first line of defense for the French at *Tiotiake* Where The People Split (Montreal). This confederacy was known as the Seven Nations Confederacy and modeled after an older confederacy, the *Wabanaké* Peoples of The Dawn confederacy.

It would be Indigenous men from the *Kenienké:haka* (Mohawk) village of *Kanehsatake* Place Of The Sand Banks which the *Anishnaabe* First Humans (Algonquins) would call *Oka* Place Of The Pickerel, that would help lead Pierre Gaulthier de Varennes and other Courier De Bois (runners of the woods) out west in 1685 and later. These Courier De Bois were both explorers and fur traders and were mainly French but had lived more like the Indigenous people. They would set the stage for the beginning of not only the *Métis* people out west, but also the distinct *Métis* Nation that would evolve.

After the war ended between the English and the French in 1760, the English representative for the Indian Department, William Johnson, secured a treaty from the Seven Nations promising that if they remained at peace with the English, they would have freedom of religion and retain the rights to the lands they lived on.

It was during that time in the year 1784, that English and Scottish merchants would form a rival fur trading company at the *Kenienké:haka* Flint People (Mohawk) place they named *Tiotiaké* Where the People Split (Montreal), and call it the North West Company. In later years some of the merchants would include United Empire Loyalists who had sought refuge in British North America after the American Revolutionary War. The North West Company was unique from the Hudson's Bay Company because their traders would go and live with the Indigenous peoples, instead of the Indigenous peoples coming to them. By 1803 the North West Company had set up a trading post at *Kitchi Gami* Great Lake (Lake Superior) and named it Fort William. In order to bring the furs back from Fort William to Montreal, they would need to rely on the best canoe men in the world. That would be the Indigenous people who knew the rivers and the Frenchmen who had lived among them.

It was from the villages of *Kanehsatake* Place Of The Sandbanks and *Kahnawaké* The Rapids that some of the best canoe men would come from. In fact *Kenienké:haka* (Mohawk) men had made sport of canoeing the treacherous waters of what had become known as the Lachine Rapids. These men and their descendants would be an integral part of what would evolve into the *Métis* Nation out west. Their first language would be *Kenienké* (Mohawk) and their second language French. Some would be involved in helping to convert Indigenous people out west to the Catholic faith. Others would intermarry with Cree women. Some had already been the offspring of Frenchmen and women from the Seven Nations Confederacy. They were of mixed heritage and well integrated in both societies.

The four *Kenienke:haka* (Mohawk) men most influential in the fur trade would be *Tenawatanahow, Karaconte, Calliou,* and *Waniyande*. Known for wearing the French sash, their offspring would make up some of the most influential First Nations and *Métis* families out west such as the Belcourts, Cardinals, Gladus, and Pelletiers. These men and others joined the North West Company in the early nineteenth century and remained there when it amalgamated with the Hudson's Bay Company in 1821 (Nicks p. 23).

It was just prior to the amalgamation of the two rival fur trading companies that the *Métis* would begin to evolve into a nation. Today, one just has to travel up Henderson Avenue in Winnipeg Manitoba, and there you will find a plaque commemorating the battle of Seven Oaks. This resulted when a man of Scottish descent named Selkirk bought land in the area and offered it to Scottish settlers from the east to settle. It was called the Red River settlement. Within a few years the *Métis* were being prohibited from practicing their way of life by Miles MacDonnell who was made head of the new territory. MacDonnell tried to stop the *Métis* from hunting, fishing, cutting wood, tried to prohibit unions between Indigenous Peoples and whites and from selling or trading pemmican (Siggens p. 17). The *Métis* wouldn't listen, so MacDonnell sent a bunch of goons to arrest them. The battle began when the *Métis* captured a boat that belonged to MacDonnell. It resulted in a gun battle where twenty Red River settlers were killed along with two *Métis*.

One of the first hero's of the *Métis* during this time was a man named Cuthbert Grant. At this time both *Métis* that is people of French and Ojibwa or Cree descent and Metis those of Scottish and Indigenous descent were involved in the fur-trade and living and working together developing their unique way of life. Cuthbert Grant had a belief that these people rooted in both Indigenous and European worlds, were more than just a people; they were also a nation. Louis Riel Sr., whose son, Louis Riel Jr. would become a famous *Métis* leader in the future, was a main spokesperson for the *Métis*. Together, they would create one of the most powerful symbols of the *Métis* Nation, known as the infinity flag. It was first displayed around 1814 and is considered the first Indigenous flag of Canada. The flag portrays a horizontal figure eight representing the blending of two cultures both Indigenous and European into one nation. The colors blue and white that make up one flag were influenced by the colors of the North West Company with the blue background standing for infinity. The other flag, red and white in color, represented the colors of the northern Hudson's Bay Company (Dorion & Préfontain p. 25). Today the blue and white flag is the predominant one and is utilized by the *Métis* Nation. It was just after the Battle of Seven Oaks that the flag was first flown.

The *Métis* Nation

As mentioned, The *Métis* are descended from the unions between French and some Indigenous fur-traders from the East and Indigenous women such as the *Cree* Human/Spirit (Illinew), *Anishnaabe* First Humans known as Saulteaux Sault St. Marie (Ojibwa) out west, and the *Dené* The People. Here is a little more of their story.

Métis roots go back as far as the first encounters between Europeans and Indigenous people. However, the *Métis* Nation evolved out west when the descendants of the unions of European fur traders and Indigenous people nationalized as one people to defend their lands against intruders from English Canada who wanted to disrupt their way of life and take away the lands they lived on. It is this unique history that separated other Metis in Canada from the *Métis* Nation. In some ways the *Métis* were continuing the battles that had been fought a century before between the English and French. What differed this time is that instead of an Indigenous people being caught in the middle between two European rivals, the *Métis* were thrust into a conflict for their own survival: a battle that has lasted into modern times.

Some Metis and *Métis* believe they should warrant the title as first born true Canadians. From the very beginning when Europeans arrived on the east coast and encountered the *Mi'kmaq* and other Indigenous societies, they inter-married with them, resulting in the first people to be born of both Indigenous and European descent. Most of these people either blended in with the French or the Indigenous society they belonged to. Unlike the French, the English rarely accepted the custom marriages between their own men and Indigenous women. That is, until after 1760 when English and Scottish traders took their trade along the *Kichisippi* Great River (Ottawa) and then pass the *Kitchi Gami* Great Lake (Lake Superior). Finally after 1821, when the Hudson's Bay Company and The North West Company amalgamated, it allowed English factors to begin trading as far as *Winippi* Muddy Waters (Winnipeg) and beyond.

Years before, the *Anishnaabe* First Humans (*Saulteaux*) had moved into the *Winippi* region of *Manitopai* Where The Creator Rested (Manitoba) replacing the *Nakota* The People (Assiniboine). The *Saulteaux* had arrived from *Bawatang* Place Of The Rapids (Sault St. Marie) in the mid-seventeen hundreds led by Chief Peguis and others. It had been at *Bawatang* that the *Ahjijawk Dodem* (Crane Clan) and *Mang Dodem* (Loon Clan) of the *Anishnaabe* separated, with members of the *Ahjijawk Dodem* traveling to the south of *Kitchi Gami* Great Lake (Lake Superior) and the *Mang Dodem* North around the lake. These were the two *Dodems* where the *Anishnaabe* leadership was chosen from. The *Saulteaux* had given the *Nakota* The People the designation Sioux from their own word *Natowaysis* Small Snakes as apposed to the *Natoway* Big Snakes (Iroquois) in the east. From that time on any one who spoke a language similar to the *Nakota* were called Sioux. That included the *Dakota* and *Lakota* peoples further south.

Over the years the *Anishnaabe* had developed good relations with the French traders. Their own pilgrimage west resulted when their prophets foretold doom if they didn't leave the East Coast. Over a 500 year period they had established themselves all the way from the Atlantic coast to the *Kichisippi* Great River (Ottawa) and then to the *Winippi* Muddy Waters (Winnipeg) where the French had established a trading post at the *Fourches* (Forks) (Benton-Benai pp. 94–102).

Once the trading post was set up, The French traders remained, intermarrying into various Indigenous groups and looking after their wives and children. Mostly Cree and *Saulteaux* women would become the mothers of the children of the future *Métis* Nation although there were some mixing with *Nakota* (Assiniboine) and Dené. When the English and Scottish men arrived after 1778, they would marry under Indigenous custom and leave their Indigenous wives and mix-blood children behind when they went back east. As the *Métis* children grew up, they sometimes adopted those called half-breed children or Metis as their own.

The *Métis* developed a distinct style of dress that would make them identifiable from both other Indigenous peoples and Europeans. It was called a capoté 'long hooded coat' with a brightly colored sash that could be used for many things including the drinking of water. The sash looked like a long scarf and was tied around the waist. It had evolved from the sashes worn by the French and *Kenienke:haka* Flint People (Mohawk) voyagers.

The *Métis* also developed their own unique language with three variants of dialects. A dialect is the same language but with variations. The language known as *Michif*-Cree utilizes the most important grammatical components of both Cree and French. It includes all the important verbs that the Cree use and the essential nouns that the French use. Because most Indigenous languages are verb based and describe things in detail and European languages are noun based and name people, places and things, *Michif* maybe one of the most developed languages in the world. Other dialects such as *Michif*-French utilize more French nouns, while another dialect *Bungee*, uses *Saulteaux* verbs and some English nouns. *Michif*-Cree and *Michif*-French were the most popular dialects spoken in the mid-west. Today, there is a renewed incentive to preserve the two main dialects of the *Michif* language (Dorion & Préfontain p. 25).

Part of the uniqueness of the *Métis* is in how they adapted aspects of both worlds into their society. For instance, the *Métis* utilized the Red River cart which was their own innovation; the birch bark canoe which was an Indigenous mode of transportation; and the York Boat based on a model once used by the Norsemen, as their main modes of transportation. The Red River cart had two large wheels that could travel over rough terrain without breaking down. What really made the Red River Cart unique is that upon arriving at a river, the wheels could be removed and the cart floated across the river. This would allow provisions to be kept dry.

The birch bark canoe on the other hand was one of the most durable modes of transportation ever invented. It could carry large loads of furs over various terrains and because it was light could be carried over portages that bypassed rapids. It could also be repaired very easily as all components of the canoe could be found in the bush. This was the common means of transportation by Indigenous societies in the east, for thousands of years. After the amalgamation of the Hudson's Bay Company and the North West Company, the York boat became an essential component of the fur trade. Based on an old Orkney design it was used primarily between the Hudson's Bay and the Forks at *Winnipi* Muddy Waters (Winnipeg). It could hold more furs than a canoe and was stronger in rough waters. The flat bottom allowed it to skim over water. However, it required great strength and endurance as men often had to row as long as sixteen hours a day.

The most important means of transportation was the horse. By the time the *Métis* began to evolve as a nation, the horse was still relatively new to the mid-west. The *Métis* became renowned for their riding skills, often out-doing other Indigenous societies in its use.

In terms of entertainment, the *Métis* are still known as great fiddle players and step dancers. Both the fiddle and dances originally came from the French and Scottish fur traders. The Métis then adapted them in to their culture (Dorion & Préfontain p. 24). There are songs that *Métis* and Cree fiddlers know that have long been forgotten in Scotland and France making them not only holders of heritage on this land, but in Europe as well.

The belief system of the *Métis* has always been Roman Catholicism sometimes interspersed with Indigenous customs, ever since Roman Catholic fur traders had followed the clergy out west. Due to their commitment to their religion and languages, it has often put them at odds with the Protestant Scottish and English traders from the east, who looked upon the *Métis* as being inferior. *Métis* leader Louis Riel would be condemned by some of the clergy and later ridiculed by historians for attempting to do something that had been achieved with success in other parts of the world. That was to propagate an Indigenous form of Roman Catholicism that would take into account the uniqueness of the Indigenous culture and the *Métis* in particular.

After Canada became a nation in 1867, Prime Minister Macdonald, himself a person of Scottish descent, wanted the west to be populated by English speaking Protestant Canadians. His vision was a Canada that was united from the East Coast to the West Coast, and the *Métis* and other Indigenous peoples were seen as an obstacle to his vision. Macdonald believed his vision could only be fulfilled by the building of a transcontinental railroad. To do so would require dealing with *Métis* rights to the land they inhabited differently than other Indigenous groups.

Since pre-confederation treaty-making had been the means to acquire lands from Indigenous peoples. This had meant following some of the principals set down in the Royal Proclamation of 1763 and the model set down with the signing of the Robinson Huron and Superior Treaties. In 1869, the Government of Canada bought all of Rupertsland which included the land the *Métis* lived on, from the Hudson's Bay Company. These lands had yet to come under treaty although soon after they would. Nonetheless, the *Métis* found themselves as squatters on lands they considered their own. Treaty making would only occur a year after the first *Métis* resistance in order to further legalize the transaction (Sprague p. 26). However, once defeated, just as the *Métis* had been excluded from treaty-making in Ontario they would be excluded out west as well.

The fact some of the *Métis* followed the buffalo hunt and were not sedentary farmers resulted in the belief that they were not a civilized society like Europeans but on the other hand could not be considered a true Indigenous people due to their mixed heritage; therefore, they were to be treated differently.

The reality was that although the *Métis* did not exclusively farm, it didn't mean they never farmed. Farming just wasn't always their main means of subsistence. Due to their skills as hunters, the *Métis* rivaled most people out west as hunters including other Indigenous societies. This made them appear to be both a dangerous and formidable opponent to the aspirations of men like Macdonald. The *Métis* had already been victorious in battles with the Dakota in 1850, proving they were capable of standing up to any group whether Indigenous or non- Indigenous. Just two years after confederation, the *Métis* would face the first of two great struggles for survival.

John Stoughton Dennis, a surveyor arrived at Red River and began to survey the *Métis* lands (Sprague p. 34). The *Métis* had followed the old French feudal system of land tenure, which meant that their lands stretched from the river bank in a rectangular fashion towards the uncut woods in the back where they placed their farms. The surveyors began surveying the *Métis* lands into square plots under the system used in Ontario. This deprived the *Métis* of their best lands and access to the river.

Louis Riel, a Métis educated in a seminary in Montreal had been asked to be the main spokesperson on behalf of the *Métis*. Louis Riel was a one eighth Indigenous person by blood quantum, nonetheless, he was *Métis* by culture. This was important in understanding what *Métis* identity represented. Being *Métis* involved more than how much Indigenous blood one had. It meant being a part of a unique culture and way of life.

Under the direction of Louis Riel, the *Métis* confronted the surveyors at Albert Nault's farm (Siggens p. 97). Albert Nault was also from a family whose Indigenous blood quantum was minimal. Nonetheless, he was considered one hundred percent *Métis*. The link for being *Métis* was in part a mixture between Indigenous and European; however, this did not necessarily qualify a person as being *Métis*. There were many Indigenous leaders that were of mixed blood lines who were not *Métis*. One example is Chief *Shingwauk* Pine Tree who had helped lead the revolt of both Metis and *Ojibwa* 'First Humans' at Bruce Mines near Mica Bay on Lake Huron in the 1840s. His father was a white fur trader and his mother an Ojibwa, yet he always identified himself as an *Ojibwa* person first, unlike his Metis brethren who he fought with. Another was Chief *Peguis* Little Chip who was said to have been found as a baby on a wood pile and then after in life brought the *Saulteaux* out west in the 1780's. What was happening around *Winnipi* Muddy Waters (Winnipeg) in the Red River region was unique. A nation was beginning to evolve out of the particular historical circumstances of a people who in turn had developed their own customs and language. A convergence had taken place around La Forche, of two very different peoples that would influence the history of the area to the present day.

The final straw for the *Métis* occurred when William McDougal, the self-appointed Lieutenant Governor of Rupertsland arrived accompanied by an armed force to take over what had previously been known as the North West Country and Rupertsland. This resulted in the *Métis* becoming armed and organized. McDougal thought he could trick the *Métis* by coming from the old southern trail through Pembina and surprise them, but the *Métis* were ready and waiting at St. Norbert. They forced McDougal to turn back (Sprague p. 35).

Originally, Louis Riel had been made secretary of the Métis National Committee and John Bruce president, until his resignation. Thereupon Louis Riel took the leadership role. There had been divisions between the *Métis* and the Metis who were more supportive of the aspirations of the English Protestants partly because of their previous affiliation with the Hudson's Bay Company in the past. In order to solidify the rights of the *Métis*, Louis Riel declared a Provisional Government and was declared president of the new Provisional Government of Assiniboia. He set out a bill of rights that would protect the rights of the *Métis* and its unique language and status and recognize the rights of other Indigenous peoples who lived in the area. He wanted a bilingual province where French, *Michif* and English would be equal, especially in the courts and legislature, and where the *Métis* could practice their form of Roman Catholicism.

Prime Minister John A. MacDonald had sent an emissary named Donald Smith to hear the *Métis* out. The Provisional Government was supposed to be a temporary solution until *Métis* rights were recognized in the Canadian Parliament. In order to avoid an immediate confrontation with not only the *Métis* but a possible one with French Canada, a Manitoba Act affirming the right of the *Métis* over a territory of two million acres of land, was passed on May 12th 1870 by the Canadian Parliament. It appeared that some of the *Métis* rights would be recognized in the new Province called Manitoba, but not all. Certain provisions such as the distribution of land had been left out to the chagrin of the *Métis* (Siggens p. 178).

The reality was, Prime Minister John A. Macdonald, did not want the Métis to have control over their own Province. He believed them to be inferior to English Protestants. Agitators like Thomas Scott gave Macdonald the excuse he needed to suppress the *Métis* and extinguish the rights they had fought for and won. Scott had been abusive to both *Métis* men and women. The *Métis* arrested him for sedition under *Métis* law. After a brief trial under the new laws of the Provincial Government, Thomas Scott was hanged (p. 163). Louis Riel would receive the brunt of the blame for the hanging but all *Métis* would pay a price.

Protestant Orangemen were in an uproar over the hanging of Scott. In order to appease them and to further his own goals, Macdonald sent in the 60th Rifles known as the Royal American Regiment, also known as the Red River Expeditionary Force, an army of 1,200 under the command of General Garnett Wolseley. As they were traveling west one of the songs they would sing by their campfires was Red River Valley which would become famous in its own right. Just before they arrived, Riel fled to Dakota Territory where he hid for a time (Sprague p. 74). The army forced many of the *Métis* to leave for Saskatchewan. Some of their best farmland, among the richest in Canada, still belongs to the descendants of General Wolseley's forces, as they moved into the homes and lands of the departing *Métis*.

Métis oral tradition tells of the soldiers abusing both *Métis* men and especially the women. Some like Elizear Goulet and Francois Guillemette were murdered (p. 74). For those *Métis* who wanted to remain, under an Order-in-Council to settle land disputes between *Métis* and settlers from the east, the land office always decided in favour of the settler, especially where surveys had not yet taken place. By 1878, most *Métis* in the Red River region were forced to find new lands to live on in the outer regions of the province they founded or in Saskatchewan (Shore p. 76).

An oral tradition told by Joe Goulet (Personal Correspondence 2012) says that when the soldiers arrived in what is now Carman, Manitoba they began surveying the land as homesteaders. Most of the *Métis* men were away on a buffalo hunt. When they returned they were told the land wasn't theirs because they didn't have deeds to the land. The *Métis* replied the soldiers didn't have one either. Almost immediately the soldiers put up a land registry office and deeded themselves the land. Because most considered themselves Orangemen, they named the nearby river, the Boyne River after the Protestant King William of Orange's defeat of the Catholic Irish at the Battle of the Boyne in 1690. The *Métis* had replaced the Irish as agitators to the Crown.

After fleeing to the United States, Louis Riel became a schoolteacher until surveyors arrived in 1885 to survey *Métis* lands in Saskatchewan. In the meantime he would be elected in absentia as representative for the district of Provencher (Sprague p. 85) for the third time in Canadian Parliament. Once again Riel was called up by his old friend Gabriel Dumont to help the *Métis* in their quest for their rights.

Name: _____   Time: _____

Learning Activity

1. From Montreal and Hudson's Bay follow the rivers taken by the fur traders?

2. Look and see if there are parallels in other places in world where an Indigenous society evolved from the relations between two diverse people?

3. What are the elements of both European and Indigenous cultures that have helped to define the *Métis*?

4. Find out more about Louis Riel and Gabriel Dumont, such as where they came from and what happened to them between 1870 and the second resistance in 1885?

Review

1. Define the meanings of *Métis*, Metis, half-breed, and Michif?

2. From the readings is there a difference between the Metis people in Canada and the *Métis* Nation out west? Give a reason a reason why you think there is or isn't a difference?

3. Name the four Mohawks who contributed to the development of the *Métis* people?

4. What contribution did the *Métis* make to Canada?

References

Benton-Benai, Eddie. (1988). The Mishomis book: *the voice of the Ojibway people.* Saint Paul Minnesota: Red School House.

Bird, Louis. (2001). *Personal Correspondence* University of Winnipeg.

Brizinski, Peggy. (1989). Knots in a String: *Native peoples and the fur trade.* Saskatoon: University of Saskatchewan.

Dorion, Leah. & Préfontaine, Darren. (2000). *Deconstructing Métis Historiography*: giving voice to the Métis people in *Metis Legacy* (pp. 13–36). The Louis Riel Institute and The Gabriel Dumont Institute of Manitoba.

Goulet, Joe, (2008). Personal Correspondence.

Milloy, John. (1988). *The plains Cree.* Winnipeg: University of Manitoba Press.

Nicks, Trudy. (1981). *Iroquois fur trappers and their descendants in Alberta.* 1981 (pp. 17–29). Provincial Museum of Canada.

Pain, Sidney. (1966) The Way North. Toronto: Ryerson Press.

Shore, Fred. *The emergence of the Metis nation in Manitoba in Metis Legacy, 2000.*

Barkwell, D. and Prèfontaine, D. (Eds.) (pp. 71–78). The Louis Riel Institute and The Gabriel Dumont Institute of Manitoba.

Siggens, Maggie. (1994). Riel*: A life of revolution.* Toronto: HarperCollins Publishers.

Sprague, D.N. (1988). Canada and the Métis, 1869–1885. Waterloo: Wilfred Laurier University Press.

ENCOUNTERS BETWEEN INDIGENOUS PEOPLES AND NEWCOMERS IN CENTRAL CANADA: *NEHIYAWAK* PLAINS CREE, WOODLAND, *OMESHKEGOWAK SWAMPYCREE*, *SAULTEAUX*, NUMBER TREATIES

Introduction

Both the Prairies and the Great Plains to the south are the same environments made up of open areas of tall grass situated in central North America. Today, there is mostly wheat grown on the Prairies. Most of the tall grass has all but disappeared. The Cree who live on the Prairies refer to themselves as *Nehiyawak* My Relations while others north of them are referred to as *Omeshkego* Swampy Cree. Living next to them was a people who arrived from the east who are known as the *Anishnaabé* also known as Ojibwa but were named *Saulteurs* Jumpers and became known as *Saulteaux* People From the Sault when they moved west permanently. Both peoples would be influential in signing treaties with the British Crown who represented Canada after it confederated in 1867. They were promised a good life for their children but this never came to pass. Much of this chapter will deal with treaties in what is now central Canada. They are rarely taught about in the education system. Without the good will of the Indigenous peoples signing them, Canada could not have become the country it is today. Ironically, all the treaties out west were not signed with Canada but rather its representative, the British Crown. Canada did not have the authority to sign treaties until 1923. (Woo p. 81) Neither did it have its own citizens until 1947. Regardless, Canada applied the terms of the Royal Proclamation to the treaties, relegating once again an inferior status to Indian claims to their homelands. It would be 1960 before Indians would get the Federal vote without have to relinquish their rights. In some ways had they been given the franchise before 1947, they would have been considered subjects of the Crown, something that would never be accepted by those who were traditional and always believed themselves to be allies of the Crown. In this chapter I have used Alexander Morris's 1880 book The Treaties as my main source. Once again the interpretation of the treaties is my own.

Preliminary

Manitoba Number Treaties

The period between the years 1871-1923 after the four eastern provinces confederated into the country called Canada resulted in eleven number treaties being signed between the *Saulteaux,* Cree, *Dené,* assiniboine and the British Crown. Even though Canada had been a country since 1867, it could not sign international treaties until 1923. Its citizens remained British subjects until 1947. The treaties took in lands from what became known later as the provinces of Manitoba, Saskatchewan, Alberta and the North West Territories. It included most of what would become western Canada. Most Manitobans don't realize they come under five number treaties let alone one number treaty which began in 1871 at the Old Stone Fort north of Winnipeg and ended in 1875 in Winnipeg, although there were amendments made to the treaties as late as 1876. Involved in Treaties One and Two were government representatives Lieutenant Governor of Manitoba Adams G. Archibald and Indian Commissioner Wemyss Simpson while Métis James McKay would be the interpreter. On the *Saulteaux,* Woodland and Swampy Cree side of Treaty One would be *Misskookenew, Kakekapenais, Nashakepanais, Kawaytayash, Wakowosh* and *Oizawekwon.* (Morris p. 316) It had resulted because the *Saulteaux* refused to allow land surveyors to move into their country without permission; however, they didn't want conflict and therefore applied for treaty believing it was their best chance of survival as a result of the dwindling buffalo herds and expanding settlement from the east.

During the earlier confrontations between the *Métis* of the Red River and mostly Scottish settlers, the *Saulteaux* sometimes sided with the Scottiish settlers that lived among them since 1812 as a result of an agreement first made between the Hudson's Bay Company and Lord Selkirk for the mere sum of 10 shillings. This included a large tract of territory along the Red River unbeknownst to the *Saulteaux* who had inhabited the area for a 30 year period. Negotiations between Selkirk and the *Saulteaux* would only occur in 1817. (p. 16) This would lead to confusion leading up to the Treaty One in 1871 as to whether the *Saulteaux* had earlier extinguished their title to the lands in question. The *Saulteaux* claimed they hadn't. By the time of Treaty One, the *Saulteaux* had their own aspirations for the lands they lived on believing it was still theirs and not settler or even *Métis* land. The Manitoba Act had even required that in order for the *Métis* to receive the 1,400,000 acres of land promised them, the *Saulteaux* and Cree would have to first extinguish their title to that land. This added legitimacy to the *Saulteaux* claim that the land along the Red River was still theirs. The Crown not wanting to take a chance and lose a legal argument or have to result in another military expedition like it had done with the Métis decided it would be better to negotiate. Both the *Métis* and the *Saulteaux* had also been concerned because in 1869 the Hudson's Bay Company had sold a huge tract of the lands they claimed to Canada for the sum of 300,000 lb, land they believed to be theirs. They questioned how a fur trading company had any rights to their lands? (Brizinski p. 86)

One of the most prominent leaders of the *Saulteaux* at the time was *Misskooknew* Red Eagle (Henry Prince) a signatory to Treaty One whom would later become renowned for helping lead an expedition of sail boats down the Nile River in 1884, to try and save a British General named Gordon in Karhtoum, Sudan, Africa. Ironically, it was sponsored by Garnett Wolseley who had forced the Métis into submission in Manitoba in 1870 and came only one year before troops were sent in to Saskatchewan to quell the Métis a second time. Henry was the son of *Peguis* Little Chip who had brought his people to *Assiniboia* later named Manitoba around 1780. The original people of the area, the *Nakota* My Relation known as *Assiniboine* Stone Boilers by the *Saulteaux* and Cree had left for the west because of a smallpox epidemic leaving the land vacant. With the arrival of the *Saulteaux* led by Chief Peguis around 1780, they would soon establish themselves along the Red River from the borders of the United States to the central regions of Lake Assiniboine, later to be referred to as Lake Winnipeg. Ironically, *Peguis* and his people fled west from *Bascatung* Sault.St Marie also to escape a smallpox epidemic. *Peguis* himself had suffered from the debilitating effects of smallpox which left his face scarred. He had also lost a part of his nose in a fight. (Sutherland p. 9)

With the advent of first the horse and then the gun, brought by fur traders or traded up the *Mississippi Valley* Long River Valley by other Indigenous societies, conflicts began to escalate among Indigenous societies. Like other Indigenous societies throughout North America, disease brought by Europeans such as smallpox took its toll on all Indigenous societies often resulting in Indigenous societies moving onto the lands of other Indigenous societies in order to escape the disease. It may have been part of the reason the *Nakota* My Relations (Assiniboine) left the area of the Red River allowing the *Saulteaux* to move in.

The Treaty One negotiations held at the Stone Fort (Lower Fort Garry) between the Crowns representative sand *Saulteaux* resulted in 160 acres of land to be given each family of five, the maintenance of schools, and three dollars for each person. Liquor was to be prohibited. They had also been promised that they would be able to hunt over the large uninhabited tracts of land included in the treaty. It was based on the premise that the land would be so inhabitable that few whitemen would ever live on it. One of the concerns that the *Saulteaux* chiefs had was that four of their Cree brothers languished in prison because they were said to have broken a contract with the Hudson Bay Company to be their boatmen and they wanted them released which eventually they were. They also wanted two thirds of the province for a reserve. (Morris p. 33) When they were promised that they would always be able to live off of the land included in the treaty, they believed that they would be sharing the lands with settlers. Oral tradition relates that they were also promised farm implements and were told that they were to seed their land or so they thought; when in fact they were to cede their land. (Louis Malcolm 2002 Personal Correspondence) Some Métis and Metis could sign on to treaty if they chose and some did. The farming implements did not arrive until five years later and the three dollars was raised to five dollars. In return, the Crown received lands from the International boundary to the Lake of the Woods, from Roseau Lake to White Mud Lake, to the mouth of the Winnipeg River, across the lower part of Lake Winnipeg to Lake Manitoba, then across crossing the Assiniboine River to the International boundary line.

Treaty Two included once again Wemyss Simpson on behalf of the Crown and on the *Saulteaux* side *Meikis, Sonsence, Masakeeyash,* Francois and Richard Woodhouse. (p. 320) It would take place at Manitoba Post, a Hudson's Bay Fort, at the north end of Lake Manitoba with many of the same promises made. The Crown was to receive all of the land from the mouth of the Winnipeg River, from the eastern shore of Lake Winnipeg to the Berens River, to the North bank of the Little Saskatchewan River, to St. Martins Lake, to the eastern and northern shore of Lake Manitoba to the mouth of the Waterhen River, to Waterhen lake, to Lake Winnipegoses, to Shell River, to the Assiniboine River, to Moose Mounatins and to the border with the United States. (p. 42) Treaty One and Two was a vast tract of territory, three times the size of the Province of Manitoba at the time, and within a few years Peguis and his son Henry's people would be forced from the little land they had left with even less gratitude from the settlers they had both fed and protected. (p. 42)

Treaty Three in 1873 also known as the North West Angle Treaty, ironically was east of Treaties one and Two and included much of Western Ontario including a tract of land in Manitoba along the east side of the Winnipeg River on lands that belonged to *Kakekapanai* and his people who was a signatory to Treaty one. Technically they should have received the higher land and payments received in Treaty Three. Treaty three, sometimes called the North West Angle Treaty offered substantially more land and money than the first two. By this time Lieutenant Governor Alexander Morris would be the Crown's representative. However, negotiations had begun as early as 1871 at Fort Francis and into 1872 which would result in a later dispute as to the actual terms of Treaty Three. During the earlier negotiations, Chief *Powasson* had someone who could read and write English take down everything that was said. This is sometimes referred to as the Paypom Treaty which stipulated that any gold or silver found by either miners or the Ojibway would result in fair compensation to the Ojibway. (Paypom Treaty – Grand Council Treaty Three) This was reneged upon during the signing of Treaty Three though there is a question as to whether the same promises were made before the chiefs signed? The Ojibway representatives included *Kaytakaypinais, Kithigaygake, Notenaquahung, Mawedopenai, Powassung, Candacomigowininie, Papaskwagin, Maynowahtauwayskung, Kitchinekabehan, Sahkatcheway, Mukadaywahsun, Mekiesies, Oosconnageist, Washiskince, Rahkieyash, Gobay, Kamatiash, Neeshotal,*

Keejeekogay, Shashagance, Shawwinabinais, Ayashawash, Payahbeewash, Rahtaytaypaootch. (Morris p. 325) The government had used a divide and conquer tactic to get the chiefs to sign by negotiation with those who were willing and excluding those who weren't. This included farming equipment and two cows, $1,500 per year for the nation, $12 for the first year per person from the original $10, ammunition and twine, a suit of clothes and coat each year for the chiefs. The chiefs had also wanted those designated as Metis to benefit as well though they were referred to as half breeds by the Crown. They wanted free travel on boat or train through their territory but were told it would be looked into. (p. 70) Unlike the Paypom Treaty before, the Crown representatives did not agree that minerals such as gold found by the Ojibway would belong to them. That is until 1888 when the Federal Government fought the Ontario Provincial government based on the argument that they should have the right to the resources having acquired land title from the owners of the land, the Ojibway. The Federal government lost the case, but had they won it could have acknowledged the legitimacy of full land title for Indigenous peoples throughout Canada. Liquor would also be prohibited in the territory. The chiefs also wanted their medals to be made of silver and nothing less. They also were to receive schools for instruction. In terms of land the treaty included around 55,000 square acres of land from the Lake of the Woods to White Dog Bay, to Rainey River, to the Lac des Milles Lacs, to the 49th parallel, and to the White Mouth River in return for the establishment of reserves that included at the most one square mile of land for a family of five. (p. 322) Of course the Ojibway didn't understand this wasn't a sharing proposition but a one sided transaction with the Ojibway being the givers and the Crown taking whatever they could and then making Canadians believe they were giving the Ojibway land to live on.

Treaty four, also known as the Qu'Appelle Valley Treaty, occurred in the years 1874 and 75 and once again Alexander Morris took the lead in representing the Crown followed by Indian Commissioner David Laird. In this treaty both Cree *Saulteaux* and Assiniboine would be involved resulting in 75,000 sq. miles of land ceded by the three Indigenous societies. This would result in the formation and appearance of the North West Mounted Police to instill Law and Order, but to eventually enforce Canadian jurisdiction over the Indigenous peoples. It was on the return trip to Fort Ellice that the treaty commissioners met a group of *Saulteaux* who had not been able to make the trip to Manitoba House during the signing of Treaty two. This was chief *Waywasecapo* and *Otamakoowewin*. It would result in the Manitoba portion of land in Treaty Four as they were from the north western Manitoba boundary with Saskatchewan. (p. 336)

During the earlier negotiations for Treaty four, there were some disputes between first the *Saulteaux* and the Cree and then the treaty commissioners as to where the treaty should be signed. The *Saulteaux* and Cree were angry because the Hudson's Bay Company had been given rights to some of their land and trade even before treaty was signed. (p. 82) In fact the tensions were so high that there was fear of a battle occurring during the negotiations and the treaty was delayed for several days. Another issue was one of the chiefs wanted any debts to the Hudson's Bay Company to be removed. Eventually the chiefs signed the agreement with the Crown with a promise that the *Métis* would be able to continue to hunt on the land. The trump card the Crowns representatives had was that American traders had come into the North West Territory and had killed 25 Assiniboine. The Crown made it clear that they were the only protection from the Americans. The Chiefs included *Kakishaway, Pisqua, Keawezauce, Kekenawup, Kuskeetewmuscoomusqua, Kaneonuskatew, Canahhachapew, Kiisicanahchuck, Kawacatoose, Kakuwistahah, Chacachas, Wahpiimoosetoosiis, Puscoos and Meemay.* (p. 334) The agreement would include lands from the border of the United States to the Moose Mountains, to two miles west of Fort Ellice and two miles west of the Assiniboine River, to the mouth of the Shell River, to the western shore of Lake Winnipegooses, to the mouth of Red Deer River, to the northern branch of the Qu'Appelle throughout the valley including the streams of Long Lake, to the mouth of Maple Creek, to the western side of the Cypress Hills and once again to the southern border. This included all rights, titles and privileges to all the lands according to the Crown. For the Cree and *Saulteaux* it was about building relationships. (p. 331) Oral tradition claims that all wealth a foot under the soil or the depth of a plow was supposed to go to the Indigenous peoples. (Cardinal and Hilderbrandt p. 63) The Cree *Saulteaux* and assiniboine received one square mile of land per family of five. The treaty stipulates that the Indigenous peoples could not sell their land without government consent. Twenty-five dollars along with a coat every three years would go to the chief and fifteen dollars for lesser chiefs. Five dollars would go to every other Indigenous person. Farming equipment and seed would also be provided and also bull, four cows, a yoke and carpentry tools, including a grindstone. A school would also be maintained on the reserve. Hunting, trapping and fishing would be allowed to continue on all lands within the boundaries of the treaty. If buildings or public works are built on reserve lands, the Indigenous peoples of the reserve were to be compensated. (Morris p. 331) Adhesions were also made for Cree, *Saulteaux* and Assiniboine peoples who were not able to make it to treaty.

Treaty Five was referred to as the Winnipeg Treaty and consisted of lands in the midnorthern regions of Manitoba. It would cover 100,000 acres of land inhabited by the *Saulteaux,* Woodland, and *Omeshkegowak* Swampy Cree Taking in the parts of the east, west and northern regions of Lake Winnipeg to Hudson's Bay. (p. 143) The treaty took place in 1875 but there were several adhesions that went into the following year. Once again it was Alexander Morris with Metis James McKay who would be the Crowns representatives in treaty negotiations. It would require a voyage by the steamship The Colville in order to reach some of the more remote regions on the lake. (p. 144) The first stop was Berens River and then to Norway House on the Nelson River. A promise was made to allow some of the Norway House Cree a reserve at Fisher River on the west side of Lake Winnipeg if they chose. On heading to Norway House, the Cree were found to be divided between Christian and Traditional from Cross Lake. Some of the Norway House Cree asked to move due to the closure of the Hudson's Bay Post. From there the commissioners traveled to the mouth of the Saskatechewan River at the Grand Rapids where they asked the community to move to the opposite side of the river with a sum of $500. to be paid to them for the move. The land in the treaty would include the *Wahpuhpuha* or the Pas which would be negotiated the following year. (p. 145) Unlike treaties three and four only 160 acres and less were offered to a family of five with all of the other terms being the same. The lands included all of land north of treaties three and four in Manitoba from Cumberland House in the west to all of the lands east of Lake Winnipeg and as far north as Split Lake. In 1876 the commissioners resumed their journey making treaty with the *Saulteaux* of Dog Head Point and once again to meet at Beren's River with those who weren't there to sign the previous year. Chiefs and councilors at Beren's River were *Nahweekeesickquahyash, Kahwahnahkeeweenin, Nakequannayyash, Peewahhoowenin,* while the Crowns representatives included James McKay and Alexander Morris (p. 347) Those at Norway House were David Rundle, *Tapastanum,* George Garriock, James Cochrane, Harry Constatau, Charles Pisquinip, Proud McKay. (p. 348). Dog Head Island and the Jack Fish would be represented by Chief Thickfoot where they were convinced to move to Fisher River on the west side of the lake where they would receive their treaty provisions the following year.

The Nehiyawak Plains or Prairie Cree

There are some scholars who say that the *Nehiyawak* My Relations or Plains Cree culture evolved around 1790 with the fur trade in Hudson's Bay. This means that some Cree moved onto the prairies on a more permanent basis from the northern woodlands somewhere during this time in order to trade furs with Indigenous groups such as the *Assiniboine* and the *Saulteaux* further south who had arrived from the east a few years earlier. They began to transition from hunting beaver to hunting buffalo. There is some truth to this claim in that Cree from the upper woodland regions of what we now call the provinces of Alberta, Saskatchewan, and Manitoba began to make permanent residence on the prairies around this time; however, this doesn't mean that they hadn't periodically move onto the region before making a more permanent move. (Miloy p. 27)

The deciding factor for the Cree in taking a more permanent residence on the prairies was the introduction of the horse in the 18th century. By the 1790's the Cree began to adapt their culture to the lifestyle of the prairies with the horse providing a quick form of transportation where they could follow the roaming buffalo herds which at that time were in the tens of thousands. Previously, they would have remained in the woodlands during the winter protected by the shelter of the trees and winds and then move onto the prairies during the summer season to hunt buffalo on foot. The sheer size and strength of the buffalo made this daunting task extremely dangerous. One earlier method by Indigenous societies in the killing of bison was to make a buffalo pound and drive them off of cliffs and then procure the hides and meat from below. This became unnecessary once they were able to follow the buffalo herds on horseback.

Once the *Nehiyawak* and *Saulteaux* began to reside on the prairies and aligned with the *Nakota,* they clashed with other Indigenous groups such as the *Dakota* and Blackfoot Confederacy including the *Piegan* and Blood raiding each other for horses and supplies.

The Second Métis Resistance and the Nehiyawak

A pivotal time for the *Nehiyawak* occurred in Saskatchewan in between 1874 after becoming signatories to Treaty Four and 1885, when many of them began to starve. With the Buffalo dwindling due to their annihilation by American Buffalo hunters paid by the government in order to starve the Indigenous peoples not living on reservations in the United States, most of the Indigenous peoples living northern of the American border ended up signing treaties with the government of Canada. The bison had no borders and therefore as they were killed off by Buffalo hunters in the south few were migrating north. In exchange for allowing white settlers to live on their land and moving onto reserves where they were promised food and other supplies by the Canadian government as established in the treaties, they soon found out that the government wasn't living up to their part of the bargain. It was a period of retrenchment by the Federal government under John A. Macdonald who was concerned with saving money. Wanting to build a railroad from the Atlantic Ocean to the Pacific Ocean money was needed to fund a railroad and therefore treaty money and supplies promised in treaty was used. When the treaty supplies didn't arrive or came too late in the year to seed the land, the Cree found they could no longer feed themselves. Some of the Plains Cree leaders like Big Bear hadn't wanted to sign treaty unless the Canadian government gave them a better deal and were therefore considered belligerent and dangerous by the government representatives.(Dempsey p. 75) When Louis Riel and the *Métis* resisted against the Canadian Government from taking away their land a second time, an army was sent in to remove them. Some of the young *Nehiyawak* warriors joined the resistance while others remained neutral and the result was several white settlers being killed at Frog Lake.(Dempsey p. 170) Even though Poundmaker and Big Bear had nothing to do with the killings a Canadian army of 8,000 soldiers under General Middleton went to arrest them anyway. Close to Battleford Saskatchewan and under the command of Colonel Otter, the army attacked Poundmaker's people who were trying to escape the conflict. Poundmaker's warriors under Fine Day were able surround Colonel Otter's men and would have easily killed them all except that Poundmaker called his warriors off allowing Otter and his men to escape. (Sluman p. 228) Poundmaker, Big Bear and One Arrow eventually surrendered resulting in them being sent to Stony Mountain Prison in Manitoba and serving several years of hard labor. After their release, they would soon succumb to the effects that prison life had on them. Eight other *Nehiyawak* warriors including their leader Wondering Spirit would be hung by the neck, making it the largest mass hanging in Canadian history. Cree leaders from Saskatchewan were forced to watch the hangings. Those *Nehiyawak* that were perceived to have participated in the *Métis* resistance would have their reserves broken up and members forced to move in with other bands that had already signed treaty meaning they lost their own treaty rights and land. (Carter p. 202)

Within a few years the *Nehiyawak* would suffer even more under the administration of Indian Affairs Minister, Hayter Reed, who had once called them the scum of the earth. When some of the *Nehiyawak* adapted to their new way of life of farming and started to become successful wheat farmers, Reed prohibited them from selling their crops on the market or for purchasing farm equipment. There had been complaints from settler farmers that the *Nehiawak* were becoming too successful. The *Nehiawak* farmers were prohibited from using any metal in their farm tools such as nails and bolts and instead were forced to make wooden farm implements by hand. Reed called it 'from peasant to civilization policy'. (Carter p. 213) Worse still, was the loss of their children to Residential Boarding Schools, where parents and children were not allowed to see one another for years on end. At the schools, some of which were the harshest in Canada, many children were abused by the clergy and nuns who ran the schools. A child could receive a beating over a hundred times with a strap if they spoke the Cree language or even have a needle put their tongues. Others suffered from being sexually abused by predators sent to work at the schools by both the government and clergy. (Miller p.329)

Previously the *Nehiyawak* had a vibrant culture and way of life. After 1885, ceremonies like the Sundance were prohibited by Canadian law until 1951. One could even be arrested if one wore traditional clothing outside or performed a traditional dance. Still, some *Nehiyawak* persevered from the Residential School and government policies and were able to use their experiences to make them stronger, even becoming successful as politicians, actors, and businessmen among other things. Like many other Indigenous societies in Canada, due to their resiliency the Plains Cree have continued to survive and in some cases are beginning to thrive.

Nehiyawak Traditional Lifestyle

As mentioned, once the Cree moved onto the prairies, the traditional lifestyle of the *Nehiyawak* required that they adapt. This included clothing, food and shelter. Typical of the type of clothing that Plains Cree men wore was the breechclout made out of deer skin. It consisted of leather that hung from a belt and fell along the sides of the legs. These were unlike pants that completely surround the leg. These allowed ventilation, protection and movement to the leg, especially when riding a horse. You have to remember that before the introduction of cloth, leather leggings were very heavy, and to have leggings that surrounded the leg especially during the summer would have resulted in overheating and lack of mobility A buffalo robe provided adequate clothing for the upper body, especially as it got colder but could be used during every season. (Mendelbaum p.81) Women also utilized buffalo robes; however, they also wore a dress that hung from two straps to the knee. Moccasins that were one piece and sowed around the feet were worn. (p. 83) During the winter they wore leather mittens. The Plains Cree created beautiful designs on their clothing out of porcupine quill. Later on they would use beads traded from other Indigenous groups who acquired them from Europeans. The most important ceremonial clothing that a man could wear and an innovation they made after moving onto the prairies was the Eagle Feather Bonnet. This was an item of clothing that had been used for thousands of years by other Indigenous groups on the Prairies. Each eagle feather that one acquired represented a great deed. They also utilized buffalo horn caps. This was a small cap with a buffalo horn on each side. Sometimes, when hunting buffalo a similar cap which covered much of the head was used. The hunter could then sneak up and make the kill. (p. 84)

Once they moved onto the Prairies, the buffalo provided much of the food supply of the Plains Cree. The Plains Cree made buffalo pounds whereby buffalo were directed into a chute and enclosure making them easy to kill with bow and arrow. The buffalo was then skinned and the choice parts eaten: these were the tongue, shoulder, heart and kidneys. The most important survival food was pemmican. It consisted of pounded meat, berries and melted fat. Once dried, it could be preserved for a long time. (p. 55)

Like other Indigenous societies living on the Prairies, the Plains Cree utilized the tipi as their main residence. These were made of three poles from the lodge pole pine that had their bark whittled off. The poles were then stood up and placed across one another at the top so that it appeared as a triangle. Deer or Moose skins were then sown together and placed as a cover over the poles much like a wrap. An opening for ventilation on the bottom of the tipi allowed for breezes to carry the smoke from a central fire in the middle of the lodge to an opening in the top. The Plains Cree also created a rectangular longhouse structure for ceremonial purposes. This type of structure had been used from the east coast to the west. (p. 88)

As mentioned before, the horse changed the lifestyle of many Indigenous peoples on the prairies. It arrived from the south in the eighteenth century. Information provided by early explorers, insist that it took a while for the Plains Cree to adapt to its use. Like the dog before, in the beginning, the Plains Cree used the horse as a pack animal, that is, until they became adept at riding it. One way of acquiring good riding horses was to steal them from the Blackfoot, another people who lived on the prairies. It was considered an act of bravery to be able to steal a horse from the Blackfoot, but not from their own people.

The Plains Cree speak what is called an Algonquin language. This means they speak a language that is similar to some other Indigenous societies, but not the same. The Algonquin language is one of eleven language family groupings in Canada. Within those family groupings are fifty other languages that are spoken. The Algonquin language is the largest grouping of languages in Canada. Some place names that we have come to know that belong to the Algonquin language family: Manitoba, Saskatchewan and Quebec to name a few. The Cree language itself is a very ancient language said to be spoken by many of the spirits within the Indigenous after world.

The Plains Cree have a very complex spiritual worldview. It is a mixture of ancient beliefs from the woodlands and newer beliefs that they acquired from other Indigenous societies when they moved onto the prairies. In the Plains Cree language, *Atayohkan* are the spirits or *Manito* that look after all of the living things that were created. For instance, there is a *Manito* that looks after the deer and one for the buffalo. Like the Woodland Cree in the north, the Plains Cree practiced the vision quest. This means going without food or water for several days until one acquired a spirit helper. They also used the conjuring lodge. This was place where a medicine man 'shaman' could speak to his *Manito* spirit helpers and receive and give advice to others.

The Plains Cree also practice a ceremony that has been done on the prairies for many years. It is called the Sundance. The Plains Cree refer to it as *nipakwe- cimuwin* the Thirst Dance. Some have also referred to it as a Rain Dance. (p. 193) This may have resulted due to an amalgamation of woodland beliefs and prairie beliefs. On the prairies, most Indigenous people revere the power of the sun. However, in the woodlands, although the sun is important, the Woodland Cree and others also celebrate the power of the thunders which cause lightening and rain. Regardless, whether calling it a sun, thirst, or rain dance, it requires personal strength and fortitude to complete the dance, as one has to dance outdoors for four days without food or water. Another important ceremony occurs in the smoking tipi. This was an all-night ceremony where participants sang and smoked their sacred pipes in offering to a *Manito* upon making a pledge. It would occur if one had a vision during a vision quest to put one on. (p. 199)

Like all peoples in the world, the Plains Cree governed themselves through a set of laws passed down from generation to generation. Leadership was chosen based on a persons' ability to take care of his family and people. There were times if qualified, where a son of a chief might be chosen after the passing of a leader; however, the qualities of a person were the main requirement for being chosen as chief. Chieftainship was also divided between civil chiefs and war chiefs. Although civil chiefs held the most responsibility over the affairs of his people, war chiefs took over the affairs of the band during times of war. (p. 106) This is what occurred during the Riel Resistance when the authority of Big Bear and Poundmaker was thwarted by Wondering Spirit a young war chief.(Dempsey p. 104) Besides the chief, there was a council that decided the affairs of the people. Besides having a war chief, there were the *Okitchitawak* Strong Hearted warriors and a society made up of the bravest known as the Worthy Young Men. An elder and spiritual leader was often chosen to oversee such activities as moving a camp. In order to bring attention to activities taking place there was also a crier that relied information to the people such as when a council was to take place. The Plains Cree had several dances that they did. Some of these like the Sun Dance, Prairie Chicken Dance, Round Dance and Bear Dance were done for ceremonial and spiritual reasons.(Mendelbaum p. 219 Others such as the tea dance were done during socializing. All of the dances had their songs that went with them. Round dance songs and dances are still done frequently. Although there are still ceremonial songs and dances done today, they are less frequent then in the past. Personal songs were also sung.

Name: _____   Time: _____

Learning Activity

1. Map out the borders of the lands in treaty five?

2. Read Treaty One and then compare it with treaties in other parts of the world?

3. Compare and contrast what the Indigenous peoples received in Treaties with what the Crown received? Who got the better deal?

4. In looking over the motivations of the Crown and then the Indigenous Peoples, then place yourself in both situations, was justice served either way?

Review

1. How many number treaties are in Manitoba?

2. What were the differences between the Crowns understanding of treaties and those of the chiefs?

3. Are there any differences in the terms of the different number treaties? If so name them?

4. Who were the main groups that signed treaties in Central Canada?

References

Brizinski, Peggy. (1989). Knots in a String: An Introduction to Native Studies in Canada. Saskatoon: University of Saskatchewan

Cardinal, Harold and Hilderbrandt, Walter. (2000). Treaty Elders of Saskatchewan. Calgary: University of Calgary Press

Carter, Sarah. (1990). Lost Harvests: *Prairie Indian Reserve farms and Government Policy*. Montreal: McGill/ Queens University Press

Dempsey, Hugh. (1984). Big Bear: *The End of Freedom*. Nebraska: University of Nebraska Press

Mendelbauim, David. (1978). The Plains Cree: *An Ethnographic Historical and Comparative Study.* Regina Canadian Plains Research Center: University of Regina Press

Malcolm, Louis.(2002). Personal Correspondence. Aboriginal Focus Programs: University of Manitoba

Miller, J.R. (1996). Shingwauks Vision: *A history of Native Residential Schools.* Toronto: University of Toronto Press

Milloy, John. (1988). The Plains Cree: *Trade Diplomacy and War 1790-1870.* Manitoba Studies in Native History: University of Manitoba Press

Morris, Alexander. (1880), The Treaties of Canada with The Indians of Manitoba and the North-West Territories in including the Negotiations. Reprint: 1991 Saskatoon: Fifth House Publishers

Sluman, Norma. (1967). Poundmaker. Toronto: Ryerson Press

Sutherland, Donna. (2003). Peguis: *A Noble Friend* Chief Peguis National Park: Canadian Cataloguing In Publication